Maya® 8
at a Glance

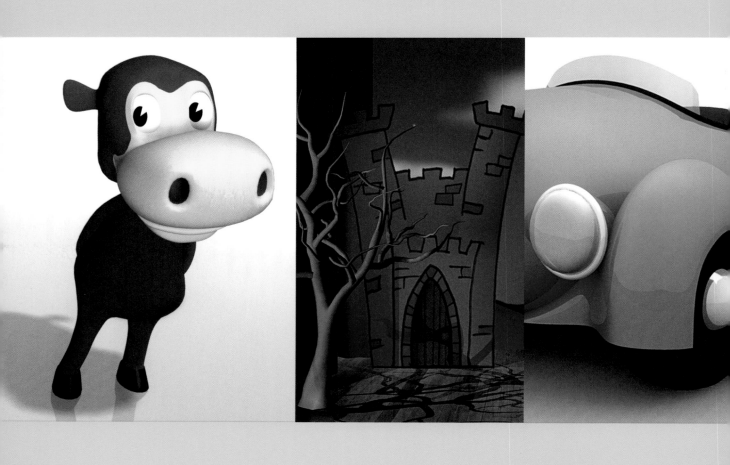

Maya® 8
at a Glance

George Maestri with Mick Larkins

Wiley Publishing, Inc.

Acquisitions and Development Editor: Mariann Barsolo
Technical Editor: Keith Reicher
Production Editor: Martine Dardignac
Copy Editor: Sharon Wilkey
Production Manager: Tim Tate
Vice President and Executive Group Publisher: Richard Swadley
Vice President and Executive Publisher: Joseph B. Wikert
Vice President and Publisher: Dan Brodnitz
Media Development Specialist: Kate Jenkins
Book Designer: Mark Ong, Side By Side Studios
Compositor: Side By Side Studios
Proofreader: Ian Golder
Indexer: Ted Laux
Cover Designer: Ryan Sneed
Cover Image: George Maestri

Dear Reader,

Thank you for choosing *Maya 8 at a Glance*. This book is part of a family of premium-quality Sybex graphics books, all written by outstanding authors who combine practical experience with a gift for teaching.

Sybex was founded in 1976. Thirty years later, we're still committed to producing consistently exceptional books. With each of our graphics titles we're working hard to set a new standard for the industry. From the writers and artists we work with to the paper we print on, our goal is to bring you the best graphics books available.

I hope you see all that reflected in these pages. I'd be very interested to hear your comments and get your feedback on how we're doing. To let us know what you think about this or any other Sybex book, please send me an email at sybex_publisher@wiley.com. Please also visit us at www.sybex.com to learn more about the rest of our growing graphics line.

Best regards,

Dan Brodnitz
Vice President and Publisher
Sybex, an Imprint of Wiley

Acknowledgments

Many, many thanks to everyone at Sybex who helped with creating such a beautiful book: Willem Knibbe, Mariann Barsolo, Pete Gaughan, Elizabeth Campbell, and Martine Dardignac. We also thank Keith Reicher, for using his Maya knowledge to keep the book technically correct, along with copyeditors Pat Coleman and Sharon Wilkey. Special thanks to Mark Ong for coming up with such a great design, and both him and Susan Riley for creating such a stunning book out of a tattered stack of text and images.

George Maestri: Many thanks to Moyet and Preston for being great kids and Margie for being so terrific. Thanks to Alex for protecting me from mailmen and squirrels. Special thanks to my friends at Tribe for answering a few sticky Maya questions and distracting me. I also thank Lynda Weinman for making the introduction to Sybex.

Mick Larkins: Thank you to Megan for all the support and love. Thanks to my family, who have always been there for me.

Thanks to all of my professors and colleagues, including John Kundert-Gibbs, Hayden Porter, Paige Meeker, Tim Davis, and Ed Siomacco.

And of course, thanks to George Maestri for allowing me to work on such an original and informative publication.

About the Authors

George Maestri has worked as a writer, director, and producer in both traditional and computer animation with 16 years of animation experience at most of the major studios. Animation is his second career. His first job, at age 16, was programming computers. He earned a degree in computer science and soon was working in Silicon Valley on high-end computer graphics systems. Being an artist and a musician, George always had a creative streak, and he ultimately left the high-technology world to study art and animation.

After working on several independent films, George got his first big break in animation in developing the pilot for *Rocko's Modern Life*, a Nickelodeon series that he also helped write. He since has also worked for Film Roman, Disney, Warner Bros., MGM, Threshold Digital, Curious Pictures, and Comedy Central, where he was one of the original producers of the hit series *South Park*. His characters "Karen and Kirby" have appeared on Kids' WB.

As an educator, George has, among his many books, published several volumes of *Digital Character Animation*, which was created as the first computer animation book aimed at artists. George has taught at Nanyang Polytechnic in Singapore, University of California Santa Cruz, DH Institute of Media Arts (DHIMA), and Lynda.com.

George is the owner of Rubber Bug, a digital animation production facility. In addition to production work, Rubber Bug develops and packages original concepts for the broadcast and educational markets.

George resides in Los Angeles with his son and daughter and Alex, the wonder dog.

Mick Larkins is currently the lead technical artist at Hi-Rez Studios and is co-author of *Mastering Maya 7*. Mick specializes in real-time animation systems and dynamic simulations. His animation and research have been presented at several prestigious animation festivals and academic conferences. He has also collaborated with several musicians and bands on various animated projects.

Mick holds an MFA in Digital Production Arts from Clemson University and a BS in computer science from Furman University. His research as a student included secondary animation techniques using cloth and hair dynamics and graphically illustrating hypothesized animal pattern formation.

Mick and his wife, Megan, live in Atlanta along with their furry friend, Fozzie. Visit Mick's website at www.micklarkins.com.

Contents at a Glance

Contents

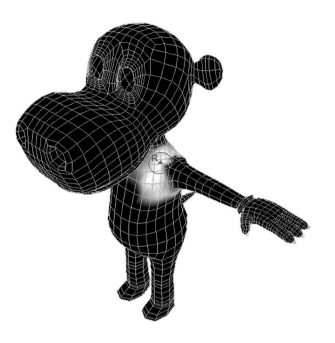

Introduction

Many years ago, I was a frustrated software engineer working in Silicon Valley. I was in a very technical field, which I enjoyed, but I also had a strong desire to exercise my artistic side. Writing code for Unix workstations just didn't satisfy that. I loved cartoons, so I decided to take the plunge and learn animation by taking some night courses at a local college. Even back then, when I was learning to draw animation a frame at a time, I found it to be a great balance of right- and left-brain activities. You could get a good creative right-brain rush by drawing lots and lots of pictures, but there were also the technical left-brain tasks of making those images move and bringing them to the screen.

As computers started to work their way into the animation world, I found that this creative/technical split became even more pronounced. People were either programmers or artists, but there were very few who were both. Soon packages like Maya came along that helped bridge that gap. Maya is the perfect package for confused right/left-brain types such as myself. Maya can be as technical as you would ever want, yet it still allows an artist to easily create stunningly beautiful images.

For the artist, learning something as technical as Maya can seem daunting, and for technical people, creating a beautiful image can be challenging. Hopefully, this book will bridge more of the gap by providing much of its information visually. Since Maya is geared toward the visual arts, we thought that a highly visual book would appeal to those who use Maya by explaining this somewhat technical topic in a visual language that is easy to understand.

This book is certainly not an encyclopedia of Maya, but as its cover says, it shows you all of the major features of Maya "at a glance." Although the book is compact, we've tried to pack a lot of good information on Maya into a small space. You should be able to flip open the book and see most of the pertinent information on a topic within a single set of pages. For those just learning Maya, we have also added tutorials at the end of each chapter to give you hands-on coverage of some of the more important tasks covered in the book. By reading through each chapter and working through the tutorials, *Maya 8 at a Glance* can also be used as in introductory course for those learning Maya.

Ideally, this book will appeal to those just getting started in Maya as well as those with experience who need a handy reference. Whatever category you fall into, I hope you enjoy *Maya 8 at a Glance*.

—*George Maestri*

What's Inside

Here is a brief synopsis of what we will cover:

Chapter 1, Introduction to Maya: This chapter gives you the basic road map so you know where things are in Maya. You'll understand the basic interface, file management, and how to navigate within the package.

Chapter 2, NURBS Modeling: NURBS are a great way to model organic shapes, and this chapter explains all of the basic tools you need to understand this modeling technique.

Chapter 3, Polygonal Modeling: Polygonal modeling is used extensively in game animation and, combined with subdivision surfaces, is used in television and feature films. This chapter presents all the tools you need to create polygonal models and subdivide them into smooth, organic shapes.

Chapter 4, Creating Textures: Maya's texture tools give you the freedom to color and shade your surfaces in any way desired. The chapter covers the creation of shaders and textures, as well as how to map those textures on a model.

Chapter 5, Lighting: This chapter covers the many methods for adding and manipulating light within the scene.

Chapter 6, Rendering: Rendering in Maya can be done using Maya's own tools or the mental ray renderer. This chapter explains all of the rendering features and effects for both renderers, including mental ray's global illumination and caustics tools.

Chapter 7, Paint Effects: Paint Effects is a 2D and 3D paint tool that can create anything from a simple brush stroke to complete 3D environments. This chapter gives you a nice overview of this very flexible and fun tool.

Chapter 8, Deformations and Rigging: Maya offers several tools for deforming meshes as well as rigging characters for animation. This chapter shows how to rig a character as well as explaining topics such as skeletons, deformers, Inverse Kinematics, and skinning.

Chapter 9, Animation: Animation brings a scene to life. The chapter covers Maya's animation tools, including the Graph Editor and Dope Sheet interfaces as well as the Trax nonlinear editor.

Chapter 10, Special Effects: Special effects artists use Maya's dynamics tools to accurately simulate reality. This chapter gives a good overview of particle systems and the forces that affect them as well as Hard and Soft Body dynamics.

Chapter 11, MEL Script: Scripting allows artists to harness the power of code in order to create custom solutions to ease work flow. This chapter provides a visual overview of Maya's powerful scripting language, MEL.

What's on the CD

The companion CD contains all the images and source files used in the step-by-step tutorials throughout the book. Use these to follow along with the instructions as you learn to try out the methods in each chapter.

If you don't already have a copy of Maya, you can install the Maya Personal Learning Edition software from the CD. Maya PLE is a special version of Maya that gives you free access to Maya Complete for noncommercial use (which means it displays a watermark on images and produces a special noncommercial file format). For hardware requirements and compatibility information, see the Autodesk website at www.autodesk.com/maya.

The Three-Button Mouse

In order to work properly, Maya requires a three-button mouse. To reference these different mouse buttons in the book, we use the following conventions:

LMB—Left mouse button
MMB—Middle mouse button
RMB—Right mouse button

Feedback

We would love to hear your feedback about this book. You can reach George through his company's website, www.rubberbug.com.

The Next Step

By the time you finish *Maya 8 at a Glance*, you'll have some solid skills for using Maya. When you're ready to move on to another level, be sure to check out other Maya titles from Sybex at www.sybex.com.

Introduction to Maya

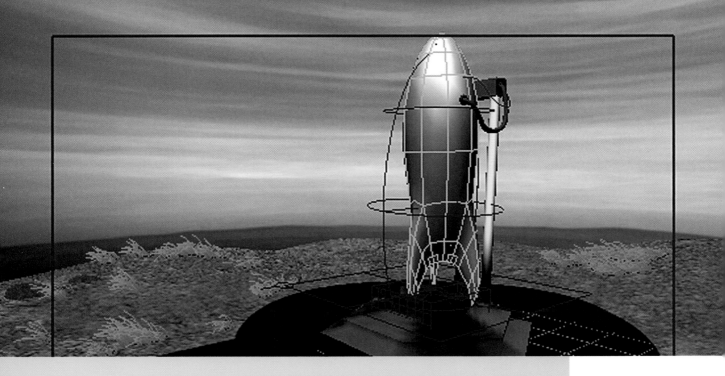

1600 x 1000

Maya is a powerful 3D modeling, animation, effects, and rendering solution that has been used in everything from product design to feature films. In capable hands, it can produce any sort of image imaginable, from an impressionistic painting to highly realistic animation and special effects.

Because of its power, Maya has a wealth of features and can seem complex at first glance. But this shouldn't overwhelm those new to the package. Getting to know a major piece of software such as Maya is much like getting to know a large city. First you need to look at a large map of the city to get a general overview, and then you explore it a neighborhood at a time. Essentially, that's how this book works. This first chapter introduces you to a general map of Maya and helps you get used to navigating the software. Subsequent chapters explore sets of features such as modeling, rendering, and animation in greater depth. When you take it a step at a time, Maya is easy to learn and use.

The Maya Interface

Knowledge of the Maya interface is the foundation of everything you will do in Maya, from creating models to texturing, animating, and final rendering. Maya offers a lot of flexibility, and you can customize it in myriad ways.

QWERTY tools Used to manipulate objects and named after their keyboard shortcuts: (Q) Select, (W) Move, (E) Rotate, (R) Scale, (T) Show Manipulators, and (Y) Repeat Last Tool.

Menu sets Let you switch between sets of menus for the tasks of animation, modeling, dynamics, rendering, and cloth.

Main menu bar Contains standard menus (File, Edit, Modify, Create, Display, Window) followed by menu items that are displayed or hidden depending on the selected menu set.

Status line Contains icons used for a number of important tasks, such as file operations, object and component selection, snapping, and rendering. Each logical group of icons is separated by a vertical bar.

Viewports Primarily used to see your 3D scenes through camera or orthographic views. Viewports can also contain data about the scene, such as with the Hypergraph or the Multilister.

Shelf A place to set your own custom tools and scripts to speed up work flow.

Channel box Contains data about the selected objects, such as position, rotation, and scale.

Layouts Instantly changes the configuration of the viewports to a number of preset layouts.

Playback controls Let you play, stop, rewind, and step through your animation.

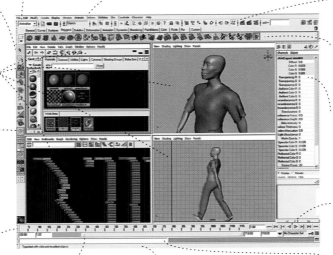

Time slider Lets you move left and right to scrub through the scene.

Range slider Limits the range of the Time slider. This is handy for long scenes, when you want to focus on a smaller segment of time.

Help line A short description of the tools and how to use them.

Command line A place to type text-based commands to Maya, such as a MEL script. Custom MEL scripts can help automate any number of tasks.

The Status Line

The Status line contains a lot of important icons that assist you with tasks such as managing files, selecting masks, snapping, and rendering options.

Menu sets Let you switch between sets of menus for the tasks of animation, modeling, dynamics, rendering, and cloth

Scene File Contains icons that let you open, save, and create new scenes

Selection masks Let you decide which components are selected when you're in component mode

Snapping functions Snap the cursor or objects to specific parts of the scene

Input/output connections Manage the way objects are connected as well as construction history

Presets A list of preset component types for use with selection masks

Selection modes Let you select by hierarchies, objects, and components

Render controls Contain icons used to render the scene and control rendering options

Name selection Lets you select objects by name or part of a name

Channel box buttons Three buttons that let you show and hide the Attribute Editor, tool settings, and Channel box

The QWERTY Tools

These tools are used for selecting and translating and are accessed primarily through the shortcut keys Q, W, E, R, T, and Y.

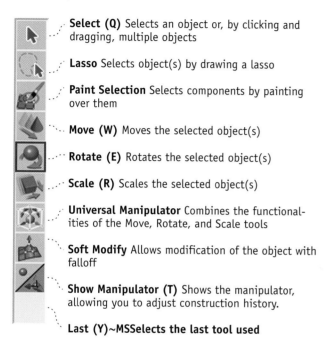

Select (Q) Selects an object or, by clicking and dragging, multiple objects

Lasso Selects object(s) by drawing a lasso

Paint Selection Selects components by painting over them

Move (W) Moves the selected object(s)

Rotate (E) Rotates the selected object(s)

Scale (R) Scales the selected object(s)

Universal Manipulator Combines the functionalities of the Move, Rotate, and Scale tools

Soft Modify Allows modification of the object with falloff

Show Manipulator (T) Shows the manipulator, allowing you to adjust construction history.

Last (Y)~MS Selects the last tool used

Layouts

The Layouts tool box quickly changes the arrangement and layout of the viewports. The viewport arrangement you choose depends on the task at hand. If you are texturing and lighting a scene, you'll want the Hypershade available. An animator will need easy access to the Graph Editor. Clicking any of the preset buttons instantly changes the views as follows:

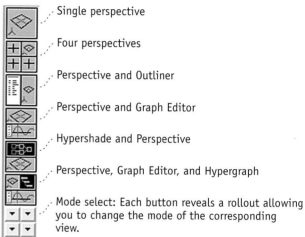

.· Single perspective

.· Four perspectives

.· Perspective and Outliner

.· Perspective and Graph Editor

.· Hypershade and Perspective

.· Perspective, Graph Editor, and Hypergraph

.· Mode select: Each button reveals a rollout allowing you to change the mode of the corresponding view.

Floating Menus

In Maya, you can tear off and "float" drop-down menus when you need repeated access to the menu. Simply left-click the double bar at the top of the drop-down.

Left-click here to float the window.

The Hotbox

Another way to easily access menus is by using the hotbox, which appears when you press the spacebar. The hotbox places all the menu commands at your cursor. You can customize the hotbox to include all the available tools or only those currently needed.

Recent Commands A list of the last tools used; handy when performing the same operations on different obejcts.

Common menus The standard menus from the menu bar.

Panel menus Menus associated with the active panel.

Hotbox Controls Lets you show and hide menus and menu sets as well as control hotbox display options, such as transparency.

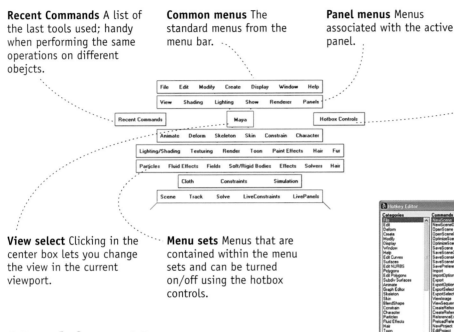

View select Clicking in the center box lets you change the view in the current viewport.

Menu sets Menus that are contained within the menu sets and can be turned on/off using the hotbox controls.

Marking Menus

Marking menus let you quickly access functions wherever the cursor is located. Once you memorize a marking menu, you can quickly select options with a simple keystroke and mouse gesture. Maya has a number of preset marking menus. You can customize the interface to your own needs using the Hotkey Editor, which lets you assign a marking menu to a particular key.

Here are a few standard marking menus:

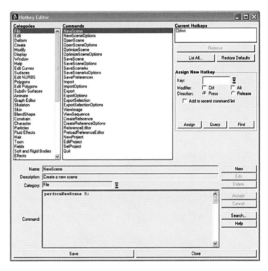

You can configure and customize hot keys and marking menus using the Hotkey Editor (choose Window → Settings/Preferences → Hotkey Editor).

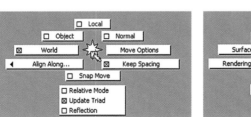

Holding down the W key while pressing the left mouse button opens a marking menu that gives you options for moving objects.

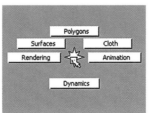

Pressing the H key selects the menu set.

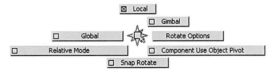

Pressing the E key displays the options for rotating objects.

The Channel Box

Clicking this button 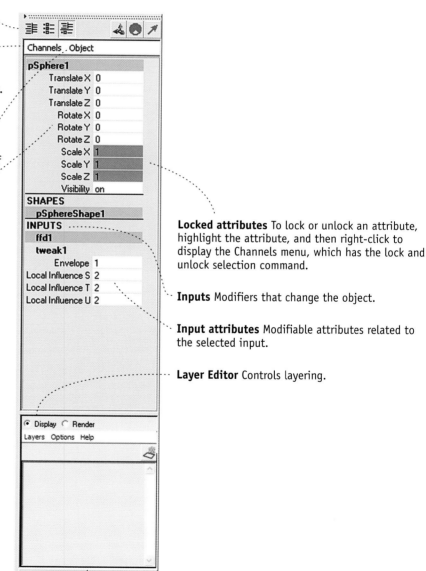, which is on the far right of the Status line, displays the Channel box. The Channel box sits along the right side of the interface and lets you quickly edit an object's main attributes. Translate, Rotate, and Scale are the most common attributes, but the Channel box provides control over many parameters of an object. It can also act as an animation interface, in which you can key parameters simply by right-clicking. You can also lock attributes so they can't be changed. This is helpful when the object needs to remain stationary, for example.

Mode Switches between Channel box, Layer Editor, or both.

Channels Drop-down menu that lets you key attributes, copy and paste attributes, and lock or unlock attributes. This menu is also available by right-clicking over the Channel box.

Object If multiple objects are selected, lets you show the individual channels of any one object.

Attributes Attributes for the object, such as Translate, Rotate, and Scale, along with others. You can change these by typing new values or by highlighting the attribute(s) and then dragging the mouse while holding down the middle mouse button.

Locked attributes To lock or unlock an attribute, highlight the attribute, and then right-click to display the Channels menu, which has the lock and unlock selection command.

Inputs Modifiers that change the object.

Input attributes Modifiable attributes related to the selected input.

Layer Editor Controls layering.

The Attribute Editor

The Attribute Editor is an important window in Maya and takes the concept of the Channel box a step further. Every object in Maya is defined by a collection of attributes, such as its position, color, shading, shape, and so on. The Attribute Editor is the interface where you can control and modify these attributes in detail.

The Attribute Editor has a series of tabs representing the nodes connected to the main object. Each node affects the object in a specific way, from altering the shape of the object to determining its shading.

Clicking this button 🖼, which is on the far right of the Status line, places the Attribute Editor on the far right of the screen. You can also open the Attribute Editor by choosing Window → Attribute Editor from the menu bar. Pressing Ctrl+A / ⌘+A also displays the Attribute Editor for the selected object.

Main menu Menus to control the Attribute Editor.

Nodes Tabs that contain attributes for each node connected to the object. These can be nodes that contain attributes used to modify the shape of the object, apply shaders, and so on.

Transform Attributes Translate, Rotate, and Scale attributes for the master node.

Pivots Lets you display a separate rotate and scale pivot.

Local/World Space Lets you adjust the rotate and scale pivots to local and world space.

Limit Information A series of rollouts that let you limit the object's translation, rotation, and scale.

Display Attributes that control how an object is displayed.

Display Handle When checked, displays a handle with which to select the object.

Rollouts Contains more parameters.

Extra Attributes Any node can contain custom attributes defined through the Attributes drop-down at the top of the Attribute Editor.

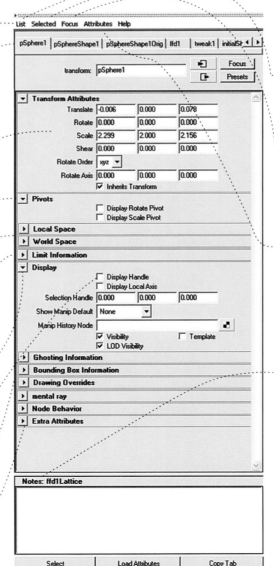

List Lets you load attributes manually or automatically when the object is selected.

Selected If multiple items are selected, lets you display the attributes of any one object.

Focus Displays all nodes that have been selected in the scene while the Attribute Editor is open. The most recently selected node is at the top of the list.

Attributes Lets you add, edit, and delete extra attributes for an object or a node. These appear in the Extra Attributes section. You can also add, edit, and delete attributes using the Modify menu.

Notes Each node can contain notes to aid in documentation.

Viewports

Viewports are where most of the work in Maya happens. Viewports can hold views of your scene as well as other types of windows that display information about your scene. The two types of views within Maya are perspective and orthographic. You select and change views using the Panels drop-down at the top of every viewport.

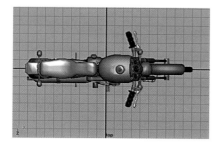 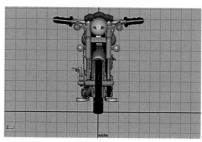 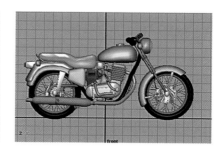

Orthographic views, such as top, front, and side views, allow only dolly and pan.

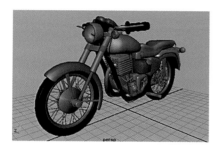  

Perspective views let the camera rotate in 3D space as well.

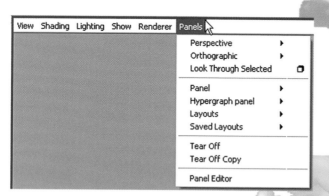

Use the Panels drop-down to change views.

Click on any axis in the view compass to quickly change views to the corresponding viewport.

Shading

Each view can have its own level of shading for viewing objects at different levels of realism. If you are creating models, you might want to view just the wireframe, but others might want to view the fully shaded and textured objects. The more realistic the shading, however, the slower the interaction; so complex scenes can bog down the system. One handy option is shading only the selected items. Not only does this speed interaction in complex scenes, it helps the selected items stand out.

The Shading drop-down on the top of the viewport controls the shading level.

Wireframe shows a simple outline of the object.

Flat Shade fills in the spaces between the wires.

Smooth Shade displays a smooth object.

Hardware Texturing displays textures. The quality of the textures depends on the graphics card.

High Quality Rendering shows advanced features such as bumps and transparency.

Navigation

To navigate within a view, hold down the Alt or Option key while clicking a mouse button.

Additionally, pressing F frames the current selection, and pressing A frames everything in the current scene.

Tumble: Alt or Option plus the left mouse button rotates the camera around a perspective view.

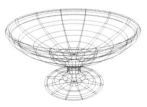

Track: Alt or Option plus the middle mouse button moves the camera left/right and up/down.

Dolly: Alt or Option plus the right mouse button moves the camera toward or away from the subject.

Selecting Objects

Objects in Maya can be NURBS (Non-Uniform Rational B-Spline) surfaces, polygonal surfaces, curves, cameras, lights, and joints, among others. Maya has three levels of selection: objects themselves, groups of objects (hierarchies), and parts of objects (components). Maya also has a sophisticated masking system that lets you select only the objects or components you want.

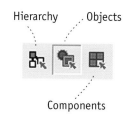

Hierarchy   Objects

Components

A group of icons on the Status line determines the selection mode.

Hierarchies

Hierarchies are groups of objects. To create a hierarchy, select multiple objects, and then choose Edit → Group. You can select a hierarchy by clicking the Hierarchy icon on the Status line, from within the Hypergraph (choose Window → Hypergraph Scene Hierarchy) or from within the Outliner (choose Window → Outliner).

You use hierarchies to logically group objects for scene management, as well as to help create complex animations. A good example is the lamp. The base of the lamp is the "root" node of the hierarchy; moving this moves the child nodes, such as the arm and the head of the lamp. Adjusting a child node, however, such as the arm of the lamp, affects only those nodes lower in the hierarchy, such as the head of the lamp.

This object is actually made of several objects...

...which are tied together in a hierarchy.

You can manage and select hierarchies of objects in the Hypergraph...

...as well as in the Outliner.

Objects

Maya supports a variety of object types, including surfaces, curves, joints, and handles, among others. To select individual objects or multiple objects, set the selection mode to Object and select with the mouse. You can also select objects in the Hypergraph or Outliner.

Using the selection masks on the Status line, you can refine object selection. By toggling the selection masks, you can select only the types of objects you want.

Handles Used to aid in the selection of objects

Curves Used to help build surfaces

Joints Used as bones to deform characters

Surfaces NURBS, polygonal surfaces, subdivision surfaces, or planes

Deformations Clusters, lattices, and other tools used to deform objects

Rendering Lights, cameras, textures, and other objects related to rendering

Dynamics Particle systems and soft bodies used for special effects

Components

You use components to modify and change the shape of an object, such as a curve or a surface. Each type of object has different types of components. A NURBS surface has components such as hulls and control vertices (CVs), and a polygonal surface has vertices, edges, and faces. Using the selection masks helps you to limit the types of components selected:

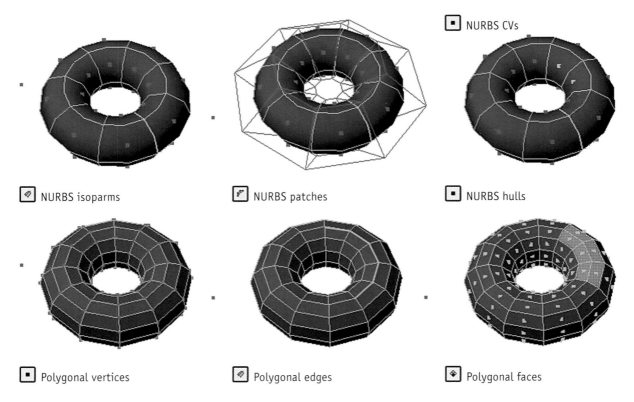

■ NURBS CVs

NURBS isoparms   NURBS patches   NURBS hulls

■ Polygonal vertices   ◆ Polygonal edges   ◆ Polygonal faces

Quick Select

sel▾ bolts

Quick Select, located on the Status line, lets you enter the name of an object to select it. This is handy when an object is in a complex scene and hard to find. Using an asterisk (*) selects all objects containing the characters, making it easy to select all similar items with a few keystrokes. For example, when selecting parts of a character, typing **Hand*** might select everything related to that character's hand. Devising and sticking to a naming scheme can help tremendously when working on large projects.

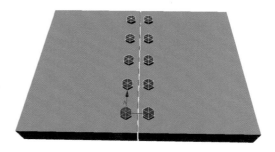

The Outliner

Another way to select objects and manage hierarchies is with the Outliner. The Outliner presents all the items in the scene as a hierarchical list. You can quickly scroll through this list to select scenes, and objects or hierarchies of objects.

To open the Outliner, choose Window → Outliner. You can also configure the Outliner to reside in a viewport using the viewport's drop-down menus.

To select an item in the Outliner, left-click it. To select multiple items, left-click and drag them. Holding down the Shift key lets you select objects in groups by clicking the first and last item of the group. Holding down the Ctrl/⌘ key lets you add or subtract items from the selection individually. You can easily rearrange hierarchies by middle-clicking the item and dragging it.

Display Drop-down menu to control how much information is displayed.

Show Drop-down menu to show and hide types of objects.

Text filter Typing a name or a global (such as bolt*) displays only those objects that match the criteria.

Root node Highlighted in green, this is the root node of the selected item(s).

Selected item Selected items are highlighted in gray.

Close hierarchy Left-clicking the minus sign (−) closes the hierarchy.

Open hierarchy Left-clicking the plus sign (+) opens the hierarchy.

Second view Moving the bar along the bottom of the screen gives you a second view of the hierarchy; useful when managing complex scenes.

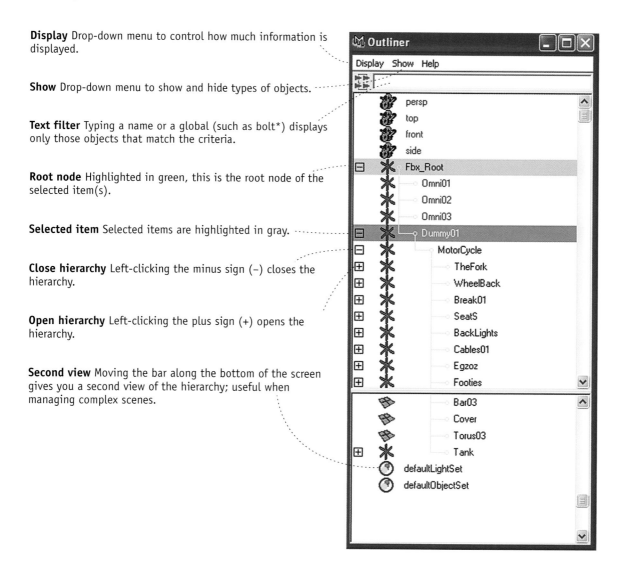

Transforming Objects

Transformations change an object's translation, rotation, and scale. These changes are stored in the object's transform node. You access the Transformation tools using the hot keys: W (Move), E (Rotate), R (Scale). You can also select these tools from the toolbox on the left side of the interface.

Each transformation tool has its own manipulator, and each manipulator is color coded. Red is the X axis, green is Y, and blue is Z. Left-clicking and dragging in the center of the manipulator moves the object on all available axes; clicking and dragging an individual manipulator transforms the object only on the selected axis. The Universal Manipulator tool combines the functionalities of translating, rotating, and scaling into one, easy-to-use tool.

> **TIP** Choose Modify → Freeze Transformations to set all your objects' current transformations at their zero positions. Choose Modify → Reset Transformations to set the transformations on selected objects back to zero, placing the objects at their origin. This resets any transformations since the objects were created or since the last time you used Freeze Transformations.

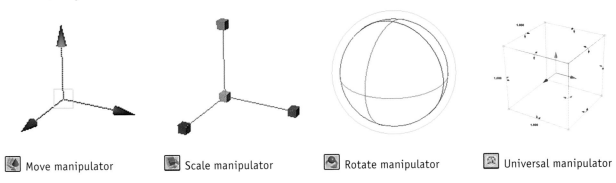

Move manipulator   Scale manipulator   Rotate manipulator   Universal manipulator

Coordinate Systems

Transformations can take place along a number of different XYZ coordinate systems. These primarily affect how an object is moved. You can change coordinate systems using the options panel for each tool.

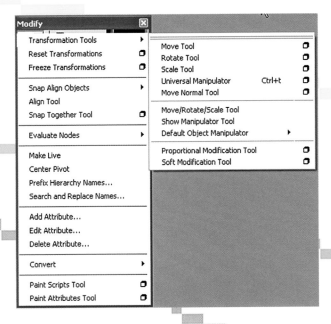

To access the options for any command, click the small box to the right of the command's name in the menu.

The Move Tool

Move tool options (choose Modify → Transformation Tools → Move Tool) select the coordinate system for the Move tool.

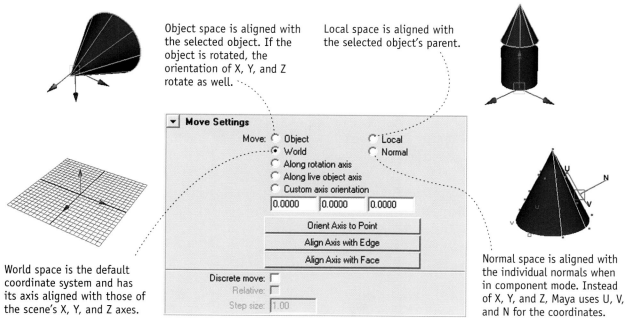

Object space is aligned with the selected object. If the object is rotated, the orientation of X, Y, and Z rotate as well.

Local space is aligned with the selected object's parent.

World space is the default coordinate system and has its axis aligned with those of the scene's X, Y, and Z axes.

Normal space is aligned with the individual normals when in component mode. Instead of X, Y, and Z, Maya uses U, V, and N for the coordinates.

The Move tool options panel

The Rotate Tool

Rotate tool options (choose Modify → Transformation Tools → Rotate Tool) select the coordinate system for the Rotate tool.

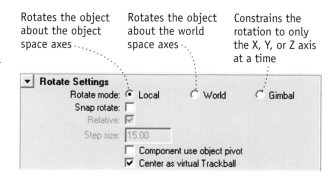

Rotates the object about the object space axes

Rotates the object about the world space axes

Constrains the rotation to only the X, Y, or Z axis at a time

Pivots

The pivot is the center of each object's coordinate system. This is particularly important when using the Rotate tool, because the object rotates around the pivot.

To adjust the placement of the pivot, press Insert or Home while in move mode. Once the pivot is in the proper location, pressing Insert or Home locks the pivot in place.

Another way to automatically adjust pivots is to choose Modify → Center Pivot. This moves the pivot to the geometric center of the object.

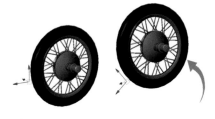

When the pivot is placed outside the wheel, the wheel rotates around the wrong center.

When the pivot is moved to the center of the wheel, the wheel rotates properly.

Connecting Objects

In Maya, every object is a collection of interconnected nodes. These nodes modify such items as the object's shape, shading, and construction history. To control the attributes of these connections, you can use the Attribute Editor, but the Hypergraph and the Connection Editor give you control over the connections and dependencies themselves.

The Hypergraph

The Hypergraph shows the contents of a scene as a network of boxes connected via lines. In this way, it functions much like a graphical version of the Outliner. The Hypergraph goes much deeper, however. Not only does it show the hierarchical connections between objects, but it also shows the way nodes and their attributes are connected.

Choose Window → Hypergraph Scene Hierarchy to open a hierarchical view of the Hypergraph, or choose Window → Hypergraph Input And Output Connections to open the Hypergraph showing the attribute connections. You can configure the Hypergraph to reside in a viewport using the viewport's drop-down menus. You navigate in the Hypergraph the same as you navigate in any view:

- Alt or Option plus middle mouse button for pan
- Alt or Option plus right mouse button for zoom

Edit Commands that let you collapse and expand hierarchies.

View Commands to frame selected objects as well as hierarchies or branches of hierarchies. These functions are duplicated with the Frame All, Frame Selection, Frame Hierarchy, and Frame Branch icons.

Bookmarks Commands to create bookmarks to easily index parts of a complex scene or hierarchy. These functions are duplicated with the Add Bookmark and Edit Bookmark icons.

Nodes Object nodes.

Graph Selects between displaying hierarchies or connections. These functions are duplicated with the Scene Hierarchy and Input/Output connections icons.

Rendering Commands used to manage and display nodes related to rendering.

Options Manage the Hypergraph.

Show Options to show and hide objects by type.

Help Help menu.

Bookmark icons Create and manage bookmarks.

Toggle freeform Toggles between freeform and automatic layout of nodes.

Display Connections icons Displays the input/output connections for the selected object.

Display Hierarchy icons Displays the scene hierarchy.

View icons Frame All, Frame Selection, Frame Hierarchy, and Frame Branch.

Text filter Typing a name or a global (such as bolt*) displays only those objects that match the criteria.

Connections Connections between nodes.

Right-clicking the body of a node displays the main Hypergraph menu.

Right-clicking along the right edge of a node displays the possible connections for that node.

Managing Hierarchies in Hypergraph

In hierarchy mode (choose Graph → Scene Hierarchy), the Hypergraph shows the objects in the scene as a tree. Each object is represented as a box, with the hierarchy represented as lines. Selecting the box in the Hypergraph also selects the corresponding item in the scene.

To modify the hierarchy in the Hypergraph, select the nodes, middle-click, and drag the line to the parent. To completely unparent a node, drag the line to an empty spot on the Hypergraph.

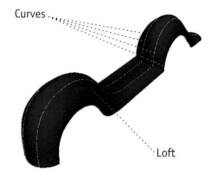

When you select freeform mode (choose Options → Layout → Freeform Layout), these boxes can be arranged in any order. This is useful for creating graphic representations of the objects in the scene, such as having the boxes represent the joints of a character.

Managing Connections in Hypergraph

The Dependency Graph (choose Graph → Input And Output Connections) is the graphical equivalent of the Attribute Editor. It lets you view the nodes that comprise objects and visualize how those nodes are connected. The Dependency Graph displays the connections for selected objects only.

Connections are created automatically as the scene is constructed. You can also make and break the connections manually to create all sorts of relationships between objects. The motion of an object along one axis can be used to drive the scale of another object, for example.

To delete a connection, click the line representing the connection and press Del. To create a connection, move the mouse over the right end of the originating node until the cursor changes, middle-click, drag to the upstream node, and release. This opens a menu, which allows you to select the parameters to be connected in the Connection Editor.

This fender is composed of four curves, which are lofted together (choose Surfaces → Loft) to create the surface.

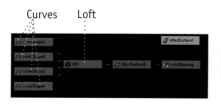

The Dependency Graph shows how the four curve nodes are connected to the loft node, which creates the surface.

Deleting the connection from one of the curves to the loft node...

...also removes it from the resulting surface.

The Connection Editor

You use the Connection Editor (choose Window → General Editors → Connection Editor) to connect attributes. It is divided into two vertical panes. Each pane contains a list of attributes from the selected objects, which can then be selected and connected using the From -> To button.

To load an object's attributes into the Connection Editor, select the object and click either Reload Left or Reload Right. To connect attributes, left-click to highlight them on each side of the window.

Loads the selected object's attributes in the left pane.

Toggles the direction of the connection.

Loads the selected object's attributes in the right pane.

Attributes Available attributes are shown in black, unavailable ones in gray.

Selected attributes The selected attributes are connected and highlighted in blue.

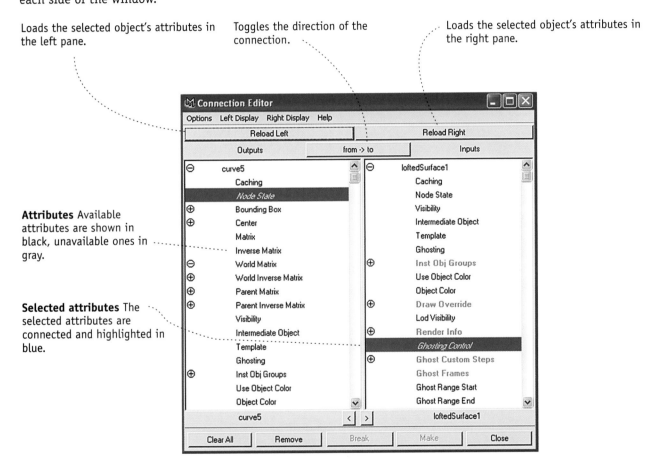

Managing Files

Projects in Maya can encompass many types of files: 3D geometry, texture maps, rendered images. Organizing these files can be a challenge, but Maya provides a standard folder structure for projects that keeps everything in the proper place. Maya is not limited to this structure, however, and you can create and store your assets in any manner you want. Productions that involve multiple artists can store all the files on a central server, for example. Assets that are used in multiple projects can be stored in their own folder structure.

Maya Folders

Each user on the system gets a Maya folder in their home folder. This allows each user to maintain their own preferences, such as custom layouts, as well as have a place for their own projects.

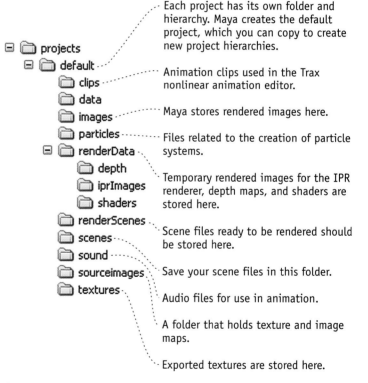

Each version of Maya maintains its own folder for installing custom preferences and scripts.

A folder hierarchy that contains Maya projects.

This is where most custom MEL scripts should be saved.

The Maya folder

Each project has its own folder and hierarchy. Maya creates the default project, which you can copy to create new project hierarchies.

Animation clips used in the Trax nonlinear animation editor.

Maya stores rendered images here.

Files related to the creation of particle systems.

Temporary rendered images for the IPR renderer, depth maps, and shaders are stored here.

Scene files ready to be rendered should be stored here.

Save your scene files in this folder.

Audio files for use in animation.

A folder that holds texture and image maps.

Exported textures are stored here.

The Maya Projects folder

Creating Projects

To create a new project, choose File → Project → New to open the New Project dialog box, in which you can define the folder locations for the project. It's always best to click the Use Defaults button at the bottom of the window, as it fills in most of the values automatically.

Name of the project.

Location of the project hierarchy.

Where the Maya scenes are stored.

Data for other components of the scene, such as textures, particles, lights, and so on. You can change individual entries to point to other places on the network, such as a shared texture library, for example.

Folders used when exporting to nonnative file formats.

Automatically fills in the entries with the most commonly used values.

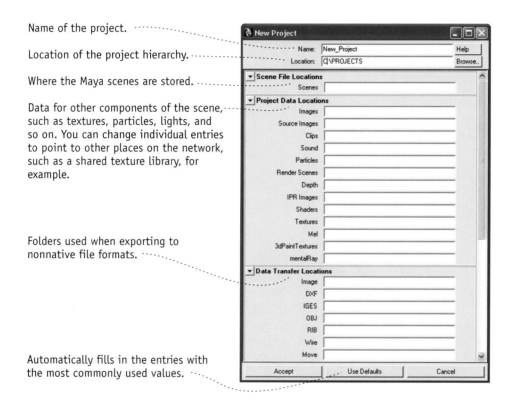

Setting and Editing Projects

To set the current project, choose File → Project → Set to open a file browser in which you can select the new project folder.

To edit the current project, choose File → Project → Edit Current to open an instance of the project window, where you can change the folders as needed.

File browser used to select a new project

NURBS Modeling

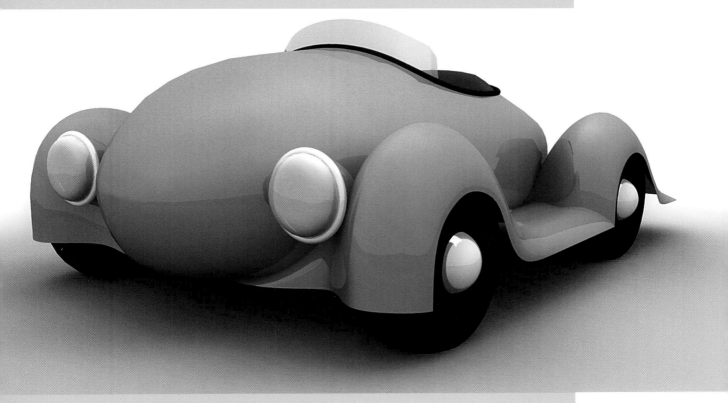

URBS modeling is exceptionally good at creating smooth, curved surfaces using a minimum of points. NURBS is an acronym for Non-Uniform Rational B-Spline, the type of curve that defines a NURBS surface.

NURBS is the first choice for automobile designers who need the precision for defining the shape of a new car. It is popular in the area of product design for creating models that have a high degree of curvature. NURBS can also be used to create deformable objects, such as characters. NURBS surfaces are excellent for creating high-resolution imagery for entertainment such as film. Because their surfaces are mathematically smooth, NURBS models can fill a giant movie screen and show no artifacts whatsoever.

NURBS modeling has always been one of Maya's big strengths. Understanding NURBS modeling is the key to understanding how Maya works.

NURBS Curves

The foundations of all NURBS models are curves, called B-splines, used to build surfaces called patches. These patches can then be tied together to create complex surfaces and models. Since they are based on curves, NURBS surfaces are naturally smooth.

Curves are primarily used to create surfaces in Maya, but they also have other applications, such as animation paths, surface deformations, and control of Inverse Kinematics (IK) chains.

A curve in Maya is built on a number of components. Control vertices (CVs) are the fundamental building blocks of the curve and are used to define its shape. Other components such as hulls and edit points can also be used to refine the shape.

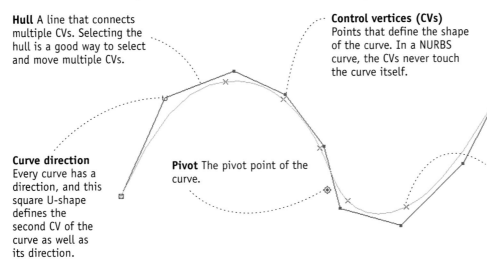

Hull A line that connects multiple CVs. Selecting the hull is a good way to select and move multiple CVs.

Control vertices (CVs) Points that define the shape of the curve. In a NURBS curve, the CVs never touch the curve itself.

Curve direction Every curve has a direction, and this square U-shape defines the second CV of the curve as well as its direction.

Pivot The pivot point of the curve.

Edit points (EPs) Points on the curve itself. These can be useful when you need to snap the surface of the curve to some other part of the scene.

Creating Curves

Curves in Maya can be created in several ways, all of which can be accessed from the toolbar or the Create menu. To draw a simple curve, select the tool and LMB in the desired viewport, clicking once for each CV or EP you want to use.

NURBS Primitives: Maya provides a circle and square primitive. You can edit these using the Show Manipulator tool or by adjusting the values in the Channel box.

Text: Text can be created in any system font, with the resulting curves used to build surfaces.

CV Curve tool: Lets you create a curve by drawing the CVs that define the curve.

Pencil tool: Creates a freehand curve by capturing the stroke of a mouse or tablet pen. To create the curve, hold down the LMB and drag while drawing the desired shape. These curves can contain a lot of CVs and be hard to manage.

EP Curve tool: Lets you create a curve by drawing the EPs that lie on the curve itself. This is helpful when you need to place points of the curve precisely.

Arc tools: Let you create a circular arc simply by placing two or three points in a viewport. You can then edit these points to adjust the curve while keeping it circular.

Curve Degrees

The degree of a curve determines how the curve will be calculated between the CVs. The higher the degree of the curve, the more CVs are used, making the curve "softer." Maya defaults to CV curves with Degree 3, which is fine for most applications. Degree 1 is great for creating sharp edges.

Curve degrees are set in the CV Curve Tool dialog box.

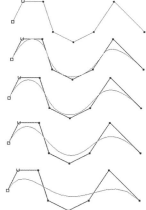

As the degree of a curve increases, the curve gets softer. From top to bottom here, Degrees 1, 2, 3, 5, and 7.

Editing Curves

Once a curve is created, you can reshape, edit, and attach it to other curves using the tools in the Edit Curves menu.

You can reshape a curve by simply entering component mode (press F8) and then selecting and moving the desired CVs or hulls. Pressing the Up or Down arrow key selects the next or previous CV on the curve.

Another way to alter the shape of a curve is to choose Edit Curves → Curve Editing Tool. The Curve Editing tool operates much like the handle of a Bèzier curve, but with a few more controls.

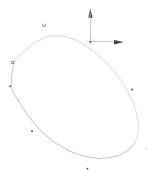

Reshaping a curve by dragging the CVs

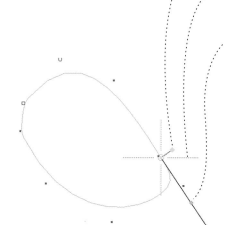

Point position Moving the point along the curve snaps the tool to the desired location.

Parameter position You can use this handle to slide the tool along the curve.

Axis Clicking an axis snaps the tool so the curve is tangent to that axis at the point position.

Tangent scale This determines the amount of "bulge" in the curve at the point position.

Tangent direction This controls the direction of the curve's tangent at the point position.

Refining Curves

In addition to basic reshaping, you can add and subtract detail from curves. You will often need to extend a curve, break it in two, or remove detail to make it smoother.

To define the point where a curve will be refined, you need to understand the concept of a curve point, which is simply an arbitrary point on the curve. Creating a curve point is as simple as turning on curve points, clicking the curve, and dragging the point to the desired location.

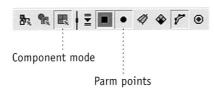

Component mode

Parm points

To turn on curve points, enter component mode (press F8) and toggle Parm points on.

Another way is to right-click the curve to open a marking menu that has an option for curve points.

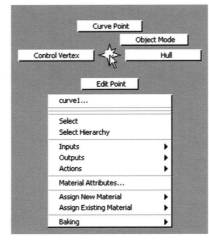

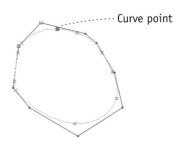

Click and drag along the curve in move mode to position the curve point.

Curve point

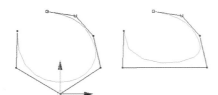

To remove detail from a curve, select the desired CV and press Del.

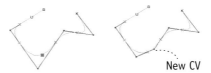

New CV

To add detail to a curve, position a curve point, and then choose Edit Curves → Insert Knot. A new CV is added at the curve point.

New curve

To break a curve in two at the curve point, choose Edit Curves → Detach Curves.

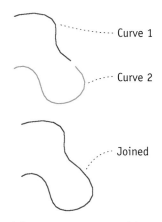

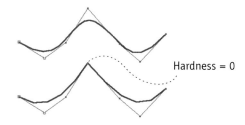

The Attach Curves menu has the option to connect the curves as one or blend them by using a third curve. When you select Blend, the blend controls appear.

To join two curves, enter object mode, select both curves, and then choose Edit Curves → Attach Curves.

Curves can be open (top) or closed (bottom). To close a selected curve, choose Edit Curves → Open/Close Curves.

Creating Corners

Typically, you use CV Hardness to create sharp edges on a CV. When you create a CV curve, the end knots default to a multiplicity factor of 3, and the arcs in between have a multiplicity factor of 1.

To harden a CV to make a corner, simply select the CV and choose Edit Curves → CV Hardness. This sets the hardness of the CV to 0, turning it into a sharp edge.

Smoothing Curves

Choosing Edit Curves → Smooth Curve simply smooths out the bumps in a curve by averaging the CVs. This is useful when a curve has been edited but is proving difficult to smooth.

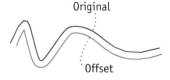

The higher the smoothing number, the smoother the resulting curve. Extremely high numbers can cause unpredictable results.

Offsetting a Curve

Choosing Edit Curves → Offset → Offset Curve creates a new curve that is offset by a specific distance. This is different from simply duplicating the curve in that the offset curve changes its curvature to maintain an equal distance from the generating curve.

Offset curves actually change curvature to remain the same distance from the original curve. Outside edges are broader, and inside edges tighter.

NURBS Patches

Think of a NURBS patch as a flexible piece of paper that can be bent and twisted into any shape. Objects can be modeled using individual patches or collections of patches that are stitched together into a seamless whole.

Like a NURBS curve, a NURBS patch is composed of many components. You can use these components to edit and manipulate the shape and surface qualities of the NURBS patch.

NURBS patches can be created from basic primitives or by using NURBS curves to define the surface of the patch. No matter what the shape, however, the patch is always four-sided.

CVs Similar to the CVs used to define a NURBS curve. Like a curve, the CVs in a patch lie off the surface of the patch and allow you to manipulate its shape.

Surface patch Defined by isoparms in the U and V direction. You can think of these as individual patches that can be copied to duplicate parts of a larger patch.

Hulls Lines that connect groups of CVs. Selecting a hull selects all CVs on the line that represents the hull. This is a good way to select related groups of CVs when editing an object.

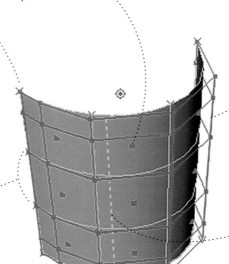

Spans The distance between fixed isoparms. Spans determine how many CVs a surface has, as well as its density.

Isoparms Cross-sections of the NURBS surface itself. Clicking and dragging on the surface of the patch displays a yellow line that can be used much like a curve point to add detail to or subtract detail from the patch.

Patches are always four-sided surfaces, which means they can have a two-dimensional coordinate system applied. Rather than the X and Y directions of a flat plane, Maya uses the terms *U* and *V* to determine the position of any point on the patch's surface. The U and V coordinates of a patch can be important when texturing a patch, as well as when modifying and refining the shape of the patch.

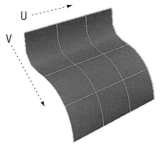

Patches are measured using U and V coordinates.

Creating Surfaces from Primitives

The easiest way to create a patch is to use the default primitives found on the Surfaces shelf or by choosing Create → NURBS Primitives. Each primitive is essentially a patch

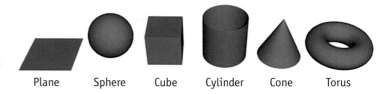

Plane Sphere Cube Cylinder Cone Torus

that is already formed into the desired shape. Primitives are a great way to begin modeling, because they can be manipulated and deformed into a number of shapes.

Building Surfaces

More-complex surfaces can be built using NURBS curves to define the surface. Using curves gives you much more precision, control, and freedom in the modeling process. If you use construction history, you can also modify the underlying curves that define a surface to animate or tweak the surface.

The Surfaces menu contains most of the functions required to turn a set of curves into a surface.

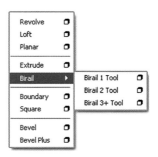

Revolve: Takes a single curve and revolves it around an axis to create a surface. Revolve allows you to specify the axis and pivot used to create the surface. As with primitive objects, you can specify the sweep and level of detail in the resulting surface.

Loft: Creates a surface using a series of curves. To create a loft, select the curves in the order you want them lofted, and then choose Loft. You can specify the number of spans between curves as well as whether the surface is open or closed.

Planar: Planar takes a curve and turns it into a surface by projecting it on a plane and trimming off the excess. In order for this to work, the curve needs to be completely flat in one dimension. Draw the curve in a front, top, or side viewport to make sure it is flat.

Extrude: Creates a surface using two curves. The first curve determines the profile of the extrude, and the second determines the path. There are options for the style of extrude and the level of detail, as well as whether the profile curves are rotated to match the curvature of the path.

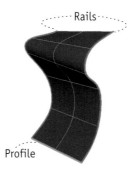

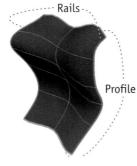

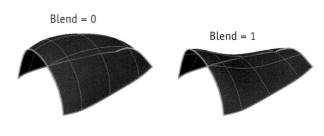

Birail 1 tool: There are several types of birail curves, which derive their name from the number of curves they use. The Birail 1 tool uses two "rails," over which is swept a profile curve. To create the surface, select the rails, and then choose Surfaces → Birail → Birail 1 Tool. The cursor changes to a heavy arrow that allows you to select the profile. In order for the tool to work, the endpoints of the profile must be snapped to the endpoints of the rails.

Birail 2 tool: Uses two profile curves in addition to the two rails. To use this tool, select the rails, choose Surfaces → Birail → Birail 2 Tool, and then select the profiles.

Birail 2 has an option to define the blend value of the curve. This allows you to make the resulting surface bulge toward or away from the profiles.

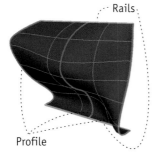

Birail 3+ tool: Uses three or more profile curves to determine the surface.

Boundary: Uses four curves to determine the surface. It's a flexible tool, because the curves do not need to be snapped together. The Automatic option allows the system to determine the best order, and As Selected uses the selection order to determine how the curves are used. Typically, the selection order is clockwise, but results depend on the selection order.

Square: Uses four curves with snapped endpoints as the outer edges of the surface. Similar to Birail 2 in its use.

Bevels: Uses a curve as the basis for a beveled edge. Choose Surfaces → Bevel to create simple rounded edges, and choose Surfaces → Bevel Plus to select a list of edge types. This tool is used a lot with text to create extruded and beveled lettering.

Refining NURBS Surfaces

After you construct a surface, you can further refine it. If history is turned on, you can manipulate the curves used to construct the surface to change its shape. You can also select the components of the surface itself and manipulate them to modify the surface's shape.

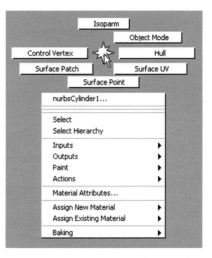

To set the point where a surface will be refined, turn on isoparms from the marking menu or the Mail toolbar.

Isoparm

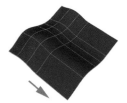

Select the isoparm. It will be highlighted in yellow. To break a surface in two along the selected isoparm, choose Edit NURBS → Detach Surfaces.

To insert an isoparm, slide the mouse along the surface until the yellow dotted line is at the desired spot for the new isoparm.

Choose Edit NURBS → Insert Isoparms to add detail to the surface.

Choose Edit NURBS → Extend Surfaces to add an extra row of CVs along the specified side.

Choose Edit NURBS → Offset Surfaces to create a second surface that is offset from the first.

Sculpting Surfaces

Using Maya's Artisan (choose Edit NURBS → Sculpt Geometry Tool) is a user-friendly way to modify and sculpt a NURBS surface. This tool uses a brushlike interface that lets you push, pull, and smooth a surface using the mouse or a pressure-sensitive tablet.

Radius The size of the brush. You can adjust the U and L size of the brush separately for oval brushes. If you use a pressure-sensitive graphics tablet and stylus, you can set an upper and lower range for the radius.

Opacity The amount of effect the brush has on the surface. A higher number strengthens the effect of the brush, which you can also control with stylus pressure.

Brushes Preset brushes to use. You can also load custom brushes by clicking the Browse button.

Operation Determines whether the brush pushes, pulls, or smooths the surface. Erase returns the surface to its original state. Auto Smooth feathers the edges of the stroke to avoid creasing.

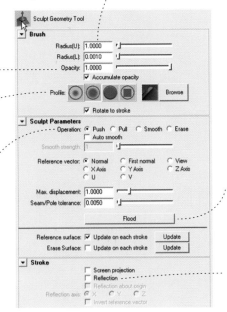

Flood Applies the brush over the entire surface. Good for smoothing the surface.

Reflection Creates a second brush that mirrors the first over the X, Y, or Z axis.

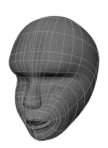

Sculpting a surface with Sculpt Geometry

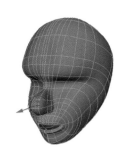

Using pull to expand the tip of the nose

Reflection lets you sculpt symmetrically.

Creating Curves on a Surface

A curve on a surface can be used to trim patches into nonrectangular shapes, to cut holes in patches, and to create a place to attach other surfaces. A curve on a surface is similar to a regular curve, except that it is constrained to two dimensions—the U and V coordinates of the NURBS surface. You can create a curve on a surface by drawing the curve directly, by projecting an existing curve, or by intersecting two surfaces.

 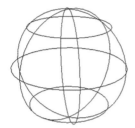 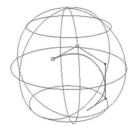 

 One way to create a curve on a surface is to draw it directly on the surface. This method gives you maximum flexibility when creating the curve. To do so, make the surface "live" by selecting the surface and toggling the magnet-shaped Make Live button on the toolbar.

When the surface goes "live," it becomes a wireframe.

Select the desired type of curve (CV, EP, or Pencil) and draw the curve as desired. You can draw as many curves as you want when the surface is live.

 Toggling live mode off ends creation mode. The resulting curves are firmly locked to the surface.

Projecting Curves on a Surface

Taking an existing NURBS curve and projecting it on a surface is useful when you need to create specific shapes or match the end curves of an existing surface to create a blend.

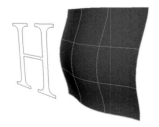 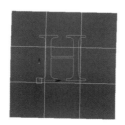 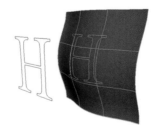

TIP Curves on a surface have a special Move manipulator that constrains the curve and its components to the surface and allows movement across the surface in U and V.

(left) Select both a curve and a surface. In this case, we're using a text outline for the curve. (center) You can project a curve along its normals or along the viewport's direction, which is usually the most direct method. To project along a viewport, highlight the top, side, or front viewport, and then choose Edit NURBS → Project Curve on Surface. The tool defaults to project along the active view, but you can change the options to project along the surface normals. (right) The result should be a curve projected directly on the surface. If construction history is on, manipulating the original curve affects the projected curve.

Creating Trims

The Trim tool uses a closed curve on a surface (or a curve on a surface that runs from surface edge to edge) as a template to trim away part of the NURBS surface. Even though the surface still exists, the trimmed area is no longer visible and will not render. Trims are useful when creating complex shapes that are difficult to model with patches.

			INPUTS	
			trim1	
			makeNurbPlane1	
			Locator U[0]	0.647
			Locator V[0]	0.637
			Selected	Keep
			Shrink	off
			Tolerance	0.001

Start with a surface that has a curve on it.

Choose Edit NURBS → Trim Tool. The surface will highlight with dark edges around the possible trim points. LMB inside the area to choose whether to keep or discard the trim points, and press Enter.

The selected area of the resulting surface is trimmed away.

If you trimmed the wrong area, you can go to construction history in the Channel box or to the Trim panel in the Attribute Editor and change the trimmed area to keep or discard the selected surface area. You can also adjust the tolerance of the trim for smoother edges.

You can trim intersected surfaces to create Boolean-like effects.

NURBS Booleans

Booleans are tools that automate the use of trims to add and subtract surfaces. The tools create a curve-on-surface at the point where the two surfaces intersect and then trim away the resulting surfaces to create the desired Boolean. Booleans are best used on surfaces that do not deform.

To create a NURBS Boolean, intersect two surfaces. Choose Edit NURBS → Booleans and the desired operation. Maya prompts you to select each surface and then press Enter.

Union Tool joins both surfaces as one.

Difference Tool removes the second surface from the first.

Intersection Tool removes all but the areas that overlap.

The Attach Surfaces Tool

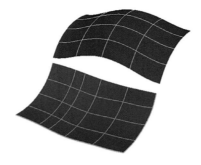

The Attach Surfaces tool joins two surfaces as one and is useful for simplifying a multipatch model. Using this tool, you can blend to join the surfaces, which smooths out the transition, or you can connect, which leaves the curvature of the original surfaces intact and can cause creasing.

Start with two NURBS surfaces. Visually align them so they are in the proper orientation. The surfaces do not need the same level of detail; Maya adds detail if it is required. Choose Edit NURBS → Attach Surfaces.

The tool creates a single surface. You can keep the original surfaces as a reference, as well as adjust the bias of the connection between the surfaces if blending is used.

The Align Surfaces Tool

The Align Surfaces tool works similarly to Attach Surfaces, but it physically moves or modifies the surfaces together so that they align at their edges. These surfaces can be attached or left separate. Using the Align Surfaces tool gives you more control over the resulting connection's curvature than using Attach Surfaces.

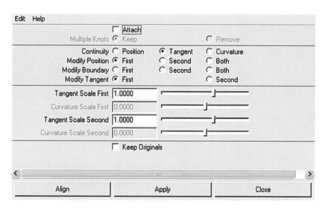

Start with two NURBS surfaces. Align them as needed. The surfaces do not need the same level of detail. Maya adds detail if it is required. Choose Edit NURBS → Align Surfaces.

The Align Surfaces tool gives you options for determining the continuity of the join whether you want to move or modify one or both surfaces. It also gives you the option to attach the resulting surfaces as one.

The final result is two surfaces exactly aligned along their edges.

The Stitch Surfaces Tool

The Stitch Surfaces tool works much as its name implies: it lets you literally sew points or edges of NURBS surfaces together to maintain continuity. You use this tool to deform surfaces and to build characters for animation.

To access the Stitch Surfaces tool, choose Edit NURBS → Stitch, and then choose Stitch Surface Points, Stitch Edges Tool, or Global Stitch.

Stitch Surface Points simultaneously stitches pairs of CVs. This tool is best used for areas where you need to do detail work by stitching only a handful of CVs.

Stitch Edges Tool stitches entire edges together. This works much faster than stitching a surface a CV at a time and is much more commonly used.

Points

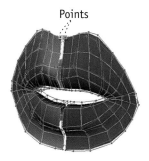

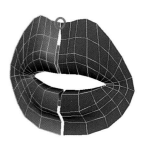

Edges

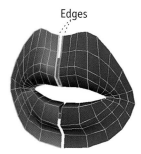

Manipulators

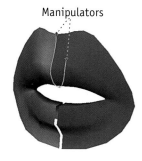

To stitch surface points, align two surfaces visually so that they are in the proper orientation. Enter component mode (press F8) and select the CVs to be stitched.

Choose Edit NURBS → Stitch → Stitch Surface Points to connect the selected points.

As with stitch surface points, you start with two aligned surfaces. Choose Edit NURBS → Stitch → Stitch Edges Tool. Select the edges you want to stitch.

The edges then stitch themselves together. At the end of each edge appears a diamond manipulator that you can select and use as a "zipper" to open or close parts of the stitch.

> **TIP** Be sure to delete history on the surfaces before stitching them.

Global Stitch lets you quickly stitch together a collection of surfaces. This is even quicker than Stitch Edges, but has no control to "unzip" a surface.

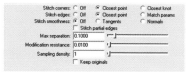

The final model is seamless and can be deformed.

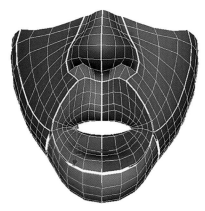

The Global Stitch tool works using the distances between edges, so you need all the surfaces aligned fairly closely.

Select the surfaces you want to stitch and choose Edit NURBS → Stitch → Global Stitch. You have options for determining the maximum distance of the stitch as well as the smoothness of the surface.

The final surface is seamless and will deform nicely.

Building a NURBS Car

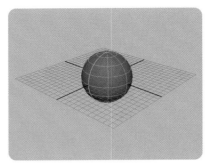

1 To start building the body, create a sphere with 8 spans and 8 sections.

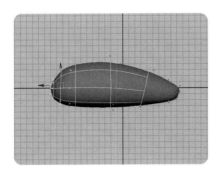

2 Rotate the sphere 90° so that the poles are pointing toward the front and the back. Go to the side viewport and start shaping the body into a torpedo by scaling and moving groups of CVs.

3 The final result should be a torpedo shape with a slightly flattened bottom.

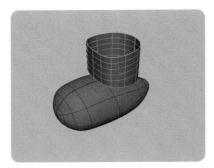

4 Next, cut the opening for the seat: create a cylinder and reshape it so that the front part is a little flatter than the rear.

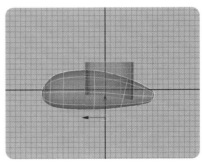

5 Slide the cylinder down so that it intersects the body. You can use the X-Ray feature (on the viewport menu).

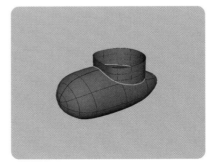

6 Select both surfaces. Choose Edit NURBS → Intersect Surfaces to create a curve on a surface at the intersection of the surfaces.

7 Using the Trim tool (choose Edit NURBS → Trim Tool), trim away the upper part of the cylinder.

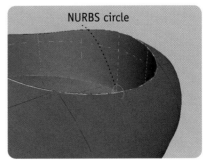

8 Trim away the shape on the body to reveal the opening. The lower part of the cylinder is the inside wall of the passenger compartment.

NURBS circle

9 Create the lip around the opening. Create a NURBS circle, and position it over the curve surrounding the lip.

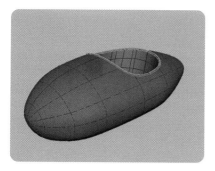

10 Select the circle, and then select the trim curve defining the edge of the opening. Choose Surfaces → Extrude. In the options, verify that the Result Position is set to At Path, that Pivot is set to Component, and that Orientation is set to Profile Normal.

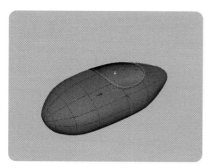

11 Create the windshield. This needs to be attached to the edge of the body opening. Select the curve representing the opening and duplicate it by choosing Edit Curves → Duplicate Surface Curves.

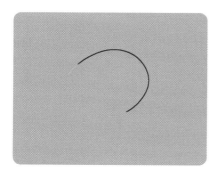

12 Select a curve point and use it to detach the curve by choosing Edit Curves → Detach Curves. The resulting curve should be similar to the green curve.

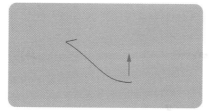

13 Duplicate this curve, scale the copy down slightly, and move it up.

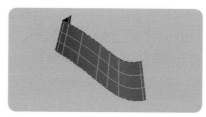

14 Use the two curves to create a loft (choose Surfaces → Loft). This is the windshield. Position it on the car body.

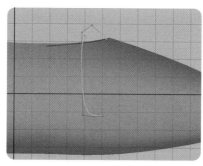

15 In the side view, create a profile of the seat.

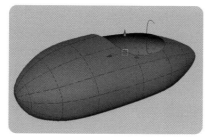

16 As you did with the windshield, duplicate the trim curve creating the opening and detach the back portion of it. If the curve splits, use Attach Curves to reconnect it. This will be the path of an extrude.

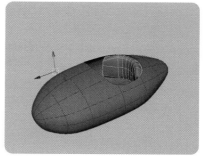

17 Select the seat profile and the path, and extrude the seat. Fit it into the opening.

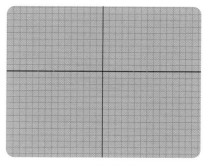

18 Now build the fenders. In the side viewport, use the CV tool to create an outline of the fender.

19 Duplicate this curve a few times and reshape the duplicates to approximate the outline of the fender.

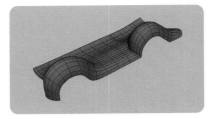

20 Loft the curves together to create the surface of the fender. If you leave history on, you can adjust the original curves to tweak the shape of the surface.

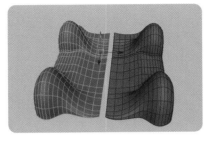

21 Create the second fender by duplicating the first fender and scaling it by –1 in the X direction.

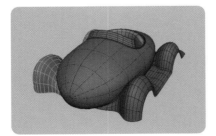

22 Adjust the fenders to fit the body of the car.

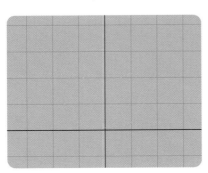

23 Create some tires. Start with a U-shaped curve that represents the profile of the tire.

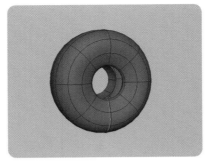

24 Revolve this curve to create the surface of the tire.

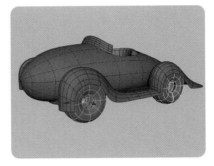

25 Duplicate the tires and fit them into the wheel wells.

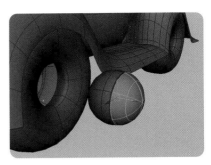

26 To model hubcaps, create a sphere, select an isoparm near the top, and detach the top of the sphere at the isoparm. Duplicate these, and fit them to the wheels.

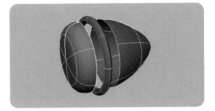

27 You create headlights in much the same way that you create hubcaps. Deform a sphere into the headlight shape, and then detach the top to make the front of the light. Add a torus as the ring.

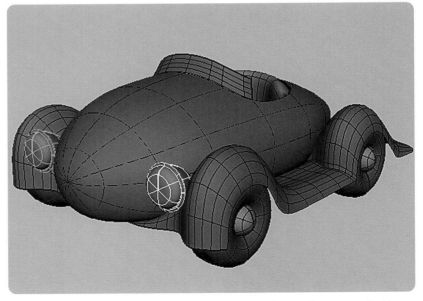

28 Duplicate and position the headlights. The car is now ready. You can continue modeling to create other details, such as door handles, taillights, and perhaps a dashboard.

Polygonal Modeling

Polygonal modeling is one of the more intuitive ways to model. Polygonal models are easy to construct and, unlike NURBS, have no topology limitations. Whereas NURBS surfaces must be stitched together from four-sided patches, polygons can have any shape or topology.

The downside to polygonal surfaces is that they are not resolution independent. Low-resolution polygonal models tend to animate quickly and are used extensively in games, but their lack of detail makes them undesirable for high-resolution rendering, such as for film or video. To overcome this limitation, subdivision surfaces allow a low-res model to be smoothed automatically at render time so that artists can get the best of both worlds. In fact, polygonal models with subdivision surfaces are quickly replacing NURBS as the standard way to create complex, deformable characters.

Creating Polygonal Surfaces

A polygonal surface is much simpler than a NURBS surface but can still define complex geometry. Unlike NURBS surfaces, a polygon is not limited to rectangular patches. Polygons can define complex surfaces without resorting to such tricks as multiple patches, trims, and blends that NURBS require. A polygonal surface can have any shape and any number of branches and still remain one complete surface in the eyes of Maya.

Polygonal surfaces have three major components: vertices, edges, and faces. To select one of these components, use the toolbar, or right-click over a polygonal surface to open a marking menu.

Edges Connect two vertices, forming a line. Edges also connect the sides of polygons.

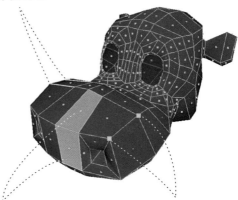

Faces Three or more edges make a face and define a plane. Most modelers stick to triangles (three-sided) and quads (four-sided), but polygons can have any number of faces.

Vertices Represent a single point in space and are the building blocks of all polygonal objects. Press F9 to enter vertex selection mode.

Creating Individual Polygons

Polygons can be created one vertex at a time. This is good for creating polygons that exactly match a desired shape or for building up complex surfaces from scratch. You can also create individual polygons to extend or modify an existing surface.

You can create a polygon by choosing Polygons → Create Polygon Tool. Each click places a vertex into the scene. You can use Snap to align the vertices to a grid or parts of another object in the scene. Pressing Enter/Return ends polygon creation mode. Add to a finished polygon by selecting it and choosing Edit Mesh → Append To Polygon Tool. Click the first common vertex, and continue clicking to add more detail; press Enter/Return to conclude.

TIP Keeping polygons planar is simply a matter of setting a preference. Choose Mesh → Create Polygon Tool ❑ and toggle Keep New Faces Planar to On in the Settings section. This keeps any new faces created on the same plane.

Keeping Polygons Planar

In geometry, three points determine a plane. Working with polygons that have more than three vertices can easily create polygons that have one vertex that is nonplanar.

You can change any polygon with more than three vertices to a nonplanar polygon simply by moving one vertex off the plane defined by three vertices. In this case, the flat plane looks like two triangles hinged together.

Nonplanar polygons will render fine but can cause problems for low-poly models used in games.

Creating Polygonal Surfaces from Primitives

Primitives are basic shapes that can be used by themselves or as the starting point for a more-complex model. To display them, open the Polygons shelf or choose Create → Polygon Primitives. Unlike NURBS primitives, which are made by deforming a patch into shapes, polygonal primitives are solid objects with no seams.

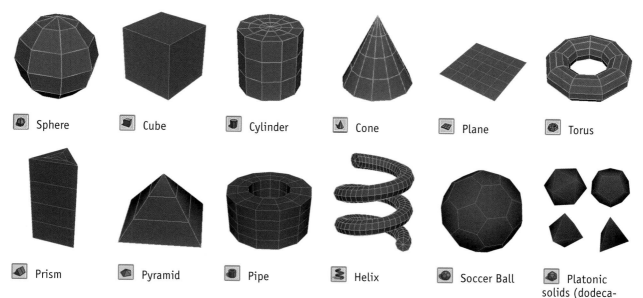

| Sphere | Cube | Cylinder | Cone | Plane | Torus |

| Prism | Pyramid | Pipe | Helix | Soccer Ball | Platonic solids (dodeca-hedron, icosahe-dron, octahedron, tetrahedron) |

Booleans

Another way to create polygonal surfaces is to choose Mesh → Booleans to add and subtract polygonal objects. The polygonal Boolean operators work much the same as NURBS Booleans (see Chapter 2), but the resulting surfaces are single objects rather than multiple surfaces. Use Booleans on objects that will remain rigid and not deform.

Boolean Difference removes one polygonal surface from another.

Combining Polygonal Objects

Polygonal objects can contain more than one surface. This allows Maya to see a complex collection of surfaces, such as the parts of a car, as one object. Combining objects can streamline the work flow, because you do not have to worry about hierarchies or grouping of objects.

By choosing Polygons → Combine, multiple objects become one single polygonal object, which can prove easier to manage and manipulate. To separate all combined objects in the polygonal object, choose Edit Polygons → Separate.

Modifying Polygonal Surfaces

Once you create a basic surface, you can modify it using a wide array of tools. You can select, move, rotate, and scale the component vertices, edges, and faces of the surface.

Adding detail to a surface through smoothing or subdivision gives you more faces and vertices with which to sculpt the surface. Smoothing and subdividing surfaces can quickly make a model dense, so be careful when adding global detail. If possible, select faces and add detail only to the areas of a model that need it.

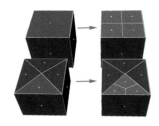

Choose Edit Mesh → Add Divisions to subdivide edges or faces. The default setting cuts each edge or edge of the face in half, but you can set the number of division levels to any desired value. You cannot subdivide faces with holes or concave faces (unless the center point is inside the face).

Choose Edit Mesh → Split Polygon Tool to specify exactly how a polygon will be split by creating new edges. You can specify the amount of subdivision for the drawn edges by changing the Divisions attribute.

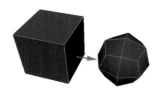

Choose Mesh → Smooth to subdivide every face and smooth it. Use the Continuity slider to determine the amount of smoothing.

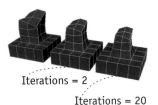

Iterations = 2

Iterations = 20

Choose Mesh → Average Vertices to smooth the surface by averaging the position of the vertices. Unlike using the Smooth command, Average Vertices does not add detail.

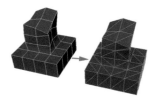

Choose Mesh → Triangulate to turn the entire mesh or selected faces into triangles. Alternately, you can turn the entire mesh or selected faces into quadrangles by choosing Mesh → Quadrangulate.

Choose Edit Mesh → Bevel to bevel the entire object or selected edges.

Choose Edit Mesh → Chamfer Vertex to expand a vertex along the intersecting edges, creating a chamfer. Width controls the chamfer size.

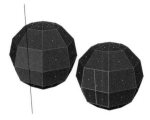

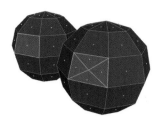

Choose Edit Mesh → Cut Faces Tool to cut selected faces along a predefined plane. You can use this tool interactively by clicking the faces and adjusting the cut plane with the mouse before pressing Enter/Return. You can also set the cut plane by typing exact values in the Attributes panel.

Choose Edit Mesh → Poke Face to subdivide the selected face so that you can move the center vertex and "poke" or "pull" the face. Good for making pointed details in a model, such as the peak of a roof.

Choose Edit Mesh → Wedge Face to select a face or faces and then an edge. The tool pivots the faces in or out, creating a wedgelike detail. It works almost like a revolve and is good for creating curves' surface details.

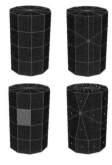

Maya provides component tools that reduce detail for creating low-poly models. To merge selected components, choose Edit Mesh → Merge; to merge components to their center point choose Edit Mesh → Merge To Center; and to merge a border edge with another, choose Edit Mesh → Merge Edge Tool. Merging components will also merge any associated UVs as well.

Choose Edit Mesh → Delete Edge/Vertex to remove the selected vertex and associated edges, while converting the remaining faces to a polygon.

Choose Edit Mesh → Delete Edge/Vertex to remove the selected edges, while converting the remaining faces to an n-gon.

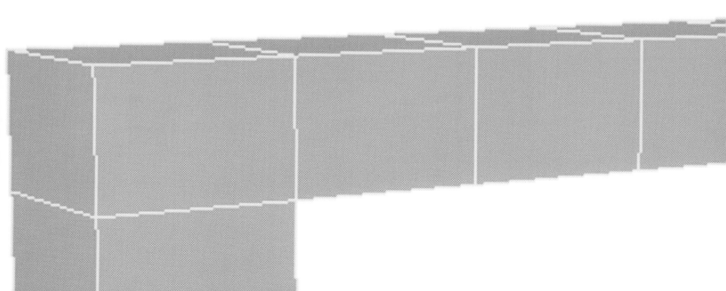

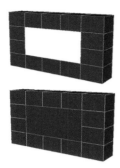

Choose Mesh → Fill Hole to fill a hole in the surface of a mesh with the selected edges. The resulting n-gon is attached to the surface, but it does not have edges; so deformations might be problematic unless you add extra detail.

Choose Mesh → Make Hole to create a hole in a polygon face. Optionally, you can create a "stamp" out of another polygon so that the hole mimics the stamp's shape. The center of the face on which the hole is made is determined by the first, middle, and last merge modes. The project merge modes make the hole exactly where the stamp face resides.

Choose Mesh → Mirror Cut to create detailed corners, such as in a picture frame or molding. The tool works by creating a mirror plane at the pivot point of the object. You can then rotate the mirror plane to create a detailed corner.

Choose Mesh → Mirror Geometry to mirror the selected detail along the specified axis. Many symmetrical models, such as human faces, are modeled one side at a time. Using Mirror Geometry is a quick way to mirror one side of a symmetrical model and create a whole.

Choose Edit Mesh → Insert Edge Loop Tool to add an edge ring to a model. These rings can be added between any adjacent rows of edges. Inserting edge loops allows you to quickly and uniformly add subdivisions to your object.

Choose Edit Mesh → Offset Edge Loop Tool to insert two lines of parallel edges on either side of the selected edges.

Extrusions

In polygonal modeling, an extrude takes a vertex, an edge, or a face and moves it away from the surface, creating additional faces that join back to the originating surface. Extrudes are useful for adding details such as limbs to a body or fingers to a hand. Select a component and choose Edit Mesh → Extrude to extrude the selected component from the mesh.

Extruding a selected vertex outward adds a pyramidal shape to tie the vertex to the originating surface. You can control the length of the extrude, the width of the base, and the number of divisions from base to tip in the Extrude options window.

You can extrude the selected edges to create new polygons.

You can extrude the selected faces to create new groups of polygons.

You can control extrudes with a curve. Select the faces to be extruded, select the curve, and then perform the extrude.

Extrude Curve Controls for the taper and twist of the extruded polygons as they follow the curve.

Taper Curve Lets you create a custom graph that determines the shape of the extrude.

Transform The size of the final polygon; usually controlled by the transform gizmo when the extrude is created.

Transform Attributes			
Translate	0.000	0.000	0.000
Rotate	0.000	0.000	0.000
Scale	1.000	1.000	1.000
Pivot	0.000	0.000	0.000
Poly Extrude Curve Attributes			
Twist	10.416		
Taper	0.744		
Taper Curve			
Selected Position	0.293		
Selected Value	0.760		
Interpolation	Linear		
Poly Extrude Face History			
Divisions	12		
Offset	0.000		
Local Translate	0.000	0.000	0.000
Local Rotate	0.000	0.000	0.000
Local Scale	1.000	1.000	1.000
Local Center	middle		
Local Direction	1.000	0.000	0.000
Random	0.000		
Smoothing Angle	30.000		
	☐ Keep Faces Together		
	☑ World Space		

Divisions Number of divisions in the extrude.

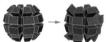

Random Adjusts the transforms of the final polygons randomly.

Keep Faces Together When off, each face is extruded separately. When on, Maya extrudes the faces together as a whole.

The Attributes panel for a polygonal extrude has options to control the size and shape of the extrude.

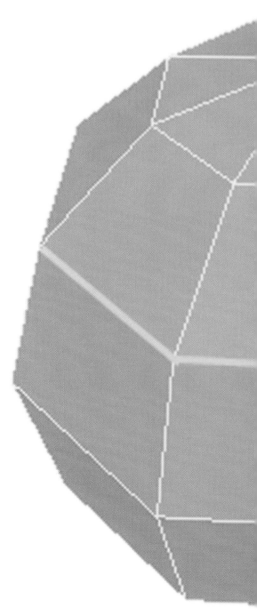

Joining and Separating Geometry

At times you will need to unify two polygonal surfaces as one. You might model a character's head separately, for example, and need to attach it to the body. Conversely, at times you'll need to separate geometry.

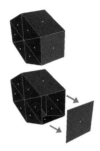

Choose Edit Mesh → Merge Edge Tool to select a single pair of edges and merge them, tying together the surfaces.

Choose Edit Polygons → Split Vertex to open a surface at the point where polygons meet at a vertex. This is good for creating holes or separating surfaces.

Choose Edit Mesh → Merge to merge selected vertices or selected faces, tying the corresponding edges and surfaces together. The vertices will merge only if they lie within a specified distance, set by a slider.

Choose Edit Mesh → Detach Component to disconnect the selected components from the mesh.

Subdiv Proxy

Typically, polygonal models tend to look rather blocky, unless they are modeled or refined to many smaller polygons. Dealing with large numbers of polygons, however, can be quite cumbersome; ideally most polygonal models should be "roughed out" using general, blocky shapes and then refined into a smoother mesh.

Subdiv Proxy allows the general shape of the low-res polygonal model to continue to drive a finer, smoother version. This capability allows you to edit your model on various levels of subdivision. In fact, subdivision surfaces work in a very similar fashion (discussed next). Conveniently, subdiv proxy models are always polygonal and are never true subdivision surfaces.

Subdiv Proxy Shader
Determines what material the proxy will use. Transparent allows you to see the new higher-res model through the low-res proxy.

Smooth Layer Display
Determines whether the smooth model's display layer will be normal, template, or reference.

Subdiv Proxy Renderable
Allows you to specify whether the proxy version of the model will be visible when rendered.

In Layer options Will separate the versions into different display layers.

Visualizing Subdiv Proxy

The Subdiv Proxy tool automatically sets up some handy visual features to aid your modeling work flow. The proxy (original) geometry can be set to keep its material or become transparent. By default, the proxy and smooth models are each placed into their own newly created layers. It is recommended to keep the smooth version in reference mode and make the proxy become partially transparent—you can edit the proxy and then immediately see the smooth version update.

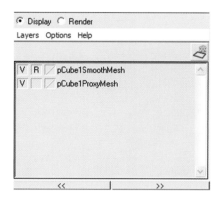
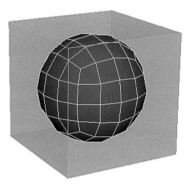

Independent from display layers, you can toggle between smooth and wire/smooth display. Choose Proxy → Toggle Proxy Display to switch between the proxy and smooth versions. To visualize both at once, choose Proxy → Both Proxy And Subdiv Display.

Adding Creases

A side effect of a subdiv proxy model is that you can easily lose creases due to the roundedness of the smoothed edges. The Crease Proxy Edge tool allows you to specify edges on the proxy that will crease the smoothed version.

Choose Proxy → Crease Proxy Edge Tool to activate the tool, and then select specific edges you wish to crease. As you MMB-drag to change the intensity of the crease, the display thickness of the edge will also change.

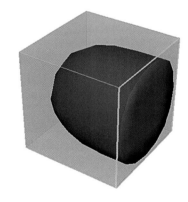

The four left-hand edges of the proxy cube were creased to their maximum strength, creating a hard crease on the smoothed model.

Subdivision Surfaces

Subdivision surfaces combine the ease of polygonal modeling with the smoothness of a NURBS surface, giving you the best of both worlds. Subdivision surfaces are used extensively in character animation because they can define almost any complex smooth surface without the need to stitch patches together.

A subdivision surface has components similar to a polygonal surface. These create a "cage" that surrounds the subdivision surface. Modifying the cage modifies the underlying surface. The surface itself can have as many as 12 levels of hierarchical detail. The base model is defined as level 0, with each subsequent refinement receiving a higher level.

Faces Much like a polygonal face, but each face has a number indicating its level in the surface.

Edges The edges of the subdivision surface help define the "cage" that surrounds the surface. Like the other components, each edge has a number indicating its level.

Vertices Vertices help define the cage surrounding the surface. Vertices are indicated by their level number.

Creating Subdivision Surfaces

Most modelers prefer to create subdivision surface objects as polygonal models first and then convert them to subdivision surfaces by choosing Modify → Convert → Polygons to Subdiv. The options include Maximum Base Mesh Faces, which needs to be set higher than the number of faces in the polygonal mesh. Depending on the complexity of the original object, the resulting surface might be represented with fewer faces. The other option is Maximum Edges Per Vertex, which controls the number of edges that can be connected to one vertex, such as at the top of a sphere.

You can also convert from a NURBS surface, but each NURBS patch is converted separately, so the resulting subdivision surfaces must be stitched together. Another route is to convert NURBS to polygons, attach the surfaces using Merge or some other tool, and then convert to subdivision surfaces.

There are six subdivision primitives available:

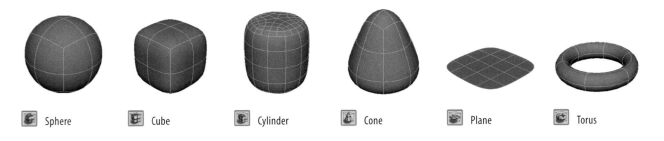

Sphere   Cube   Cylinder   Cone   Plane   Torus

Display Smoothness

As with NURBS surfaces, there are three display modes of smoothness with subdivision models. When you first create a subdivision surface, it uses the lowest mode of display smoothness. By pressing 1 (roughest), 2, or 3 (smoothest), you can change the display smoothness. You can also change this value in the Attribute Editor under Subdiv Surface Display.

It is important to note that these "modes" of smoothness are different and completely independent from the subdivision levels. Display smoothness changes only the real-time feedback quality and makes no visual difference when rendered.

Subdivision Surface Attributes

Once created, each subdivision surface has attributes to control how the surface is displayed and rendered. You can use these attributes to optimize the surface for both interactivity and final rendering.

Toggles the display of each component type on and off.

Determines how fine a mesh to display in the viewport. Resolution determines the number of subdivisions. The higher the resolution, the slower the model will be to deform.

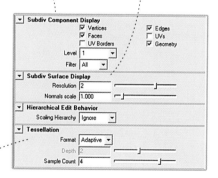

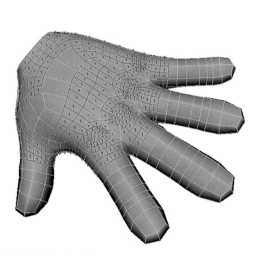

Multiple levels of detail can exist on a subdivision surface.

Determines the tessellation algorithm to use. Uniform simply subdivides the mesh evenly; Adaptive subdivides based on curvature.

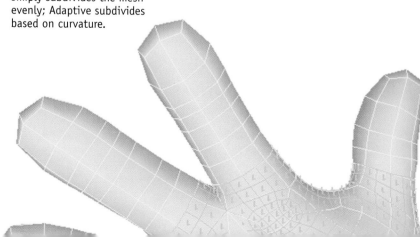

Modes

Subdivision surfaces have two modes, polygon proxy and standard. To access these modes, use the marking menu or the Subdiv Surfaces menu.

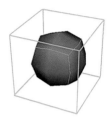 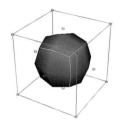

Polygon proxy mode lets you model and manipulate the base (level 0) cage surrounding the subdivision surface using Maya's polygonal modeling tools. This is the preferred method for modeling because it allows a wide array of polygonal tools along with the ability to see the final surface as it's modeled.

Standard mode lets you navigate the hierarchy of the subdivision surface. You can manipulate the components of the surface as well as add detail.

Working with Levels

Using levels is a great way to add local detail to a model. As mentioned earlier, Maya allows for a maximum of 12 levels in a model, though most models never get beyond 2 or 3 levels. Levels are set up automatically by Maya as the surface is refined. To navigate levels, choose Subdiv Surfaces → Component Display Level or in the marking menu select either Finer or Coarser.

Level 0 is the base level of the mesh and equivalent to the detail of the surrounding cage.

Level 1 contains only the detail needed to define the parts of the model that are more tightly curved.

Adding Creases

At times you need to create a hard edge on a subdivision surface. You control this process by selecting the desired vertices or edges within standard mode and using the three creasing options, which are located in the Subdiv Surfaces menu.

Full Crease Edge/Vertex causes the parts of the surface defined by the selected edges to be at a right angle.

Partial Crease Edge/Vertex rounds off the parts surface defined by the selected edges.

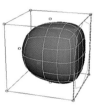

Uncreased Edge/Vertex is the default for a surface, but creased edges can be uncreased using this menu option.

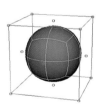

Mirroring and Attaching

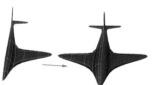 

Choose Subdiv Surfaces → Mirror to create a mirror image of the subdivision surface. This command is useful for creating symmetrical models, such as this airplane body.

Choosing Subdiv Surfaces → Attach is similar to choosing the Merge tool and lets you attach subdivision surfaces together.

Modeling a Cartoon Character

Modeling a Cartoon Character

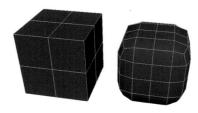

1 Let's work on the head first. Create a polygonal cube with two subdivisions on each axis. Choose Mesh → Smooth to round it off and add detail.

2 Using the marking menu, enter vertex edit mode. Start selecting vertices, and reshape the model into a rough approximation of the cow's nose.

3 Select the faces at the base of the nose and extrude them by choosing Edit Mesh → Extrude. Be sure to toggle Keep Faces Together in the Channel box. Scale and rotate the extruded faces to start forming the outline of the head.

4 Keeping the same faces selected, perform another extrude to give the head more detail. Select vertices and refine the shape of the head.

5 Once the head is reshaped, start working on the eyes. Select the four faces representing the eye socket and remove them by pressing Del. This creates a hole in the mesh.

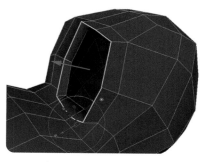

6 Select the edges around the hole and extrude them forward to create detail for the eye.

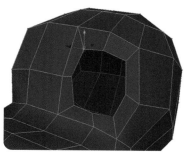

7 Select the vertices surrounding the eye socket, and reshape the newly created detail to form the outline of the eye.

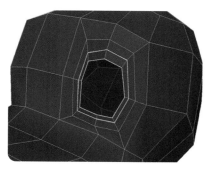

8 Extrude the edges surrounding the eye socket two more times and reshape the new detail.

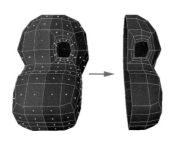

9 Select the faces representing the half of the head opposite the eye socket, and delete them. We will model only half the head for the next few steps to ensure symmetry.

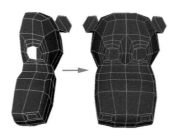

10 Create a sphere, and adjust its size and position to match the eye socket. Use this as a guide for final tweaking of the eye socket shape.

13 Once you're happy with the shape of the head, you can create the other half so you can put it back together. Choose Mesh → Mirror Geometry to create the other half of the head.

16 Rotate faces and continue to extrude until the mouth flap is complete.

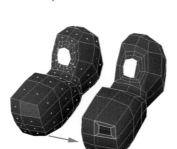

11 Create a nostril by selecting the face on the top-most corner of the front of the nose and extruding it twice. Reshape the detail to create a nostril that looks similar to the image.

14 Select the vertices along the middle of the model. Choose Edit Mesh → Merge. If all the vertices don't merge, go into the Attributes panel and adjust the Distance slider under Merge Vertex History until they all snap together.

17 Reshape and add detail to finish the mouth. The head is now almost complete. Touch up the model and refine it until you're happy with it.

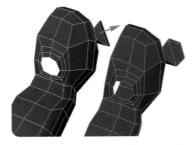

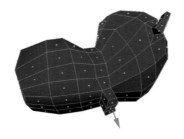

12 Create an ear by extruding a face on the side of the skull and reshaping it. You might need to rotate and scale the detail a bit to get the correct profile.

15 To create the mouth, select faces on the underside of the head, where the nose meets the skull, and extrude them.

18 Now we move to modeling the body. Start with a polygonal cube. Make it slightly taller in height. Add three rows each in Subdivisions Width and Depth and four rows in Subdivisions Height. This will give you enough detail to model arms and legs.

19 Select the middle two faces on the bottom of the model. Choose Edit Mesh → Extrude. This is the start of the character's legs.

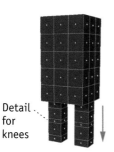

Detail for knees

20 Continue extruding the legs. Be sure to give enough detail around the knees so that they can bend smoothly. Don't worry that the legs are square; they will round out when we turn the model into a subdivision surface.

21 Create the arms in much the same manner as the legs. Select faces along the top of the sides of the body and extrude them. Be sure to give enough detail for the character's elbows so they deform properly.

22 Start sculpting the body by selecting the vertices along the outside corners and scaling them down. This rounds off the corners of the model. Continue to round the model.

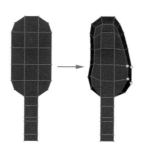

23 In the side view, model the profile of the character. Bulge out the belly a bit and straighten out the back. Continue sculpting the body.

24 Select the faces at the bottom of the legs and extrude them slightly to make the hooves.

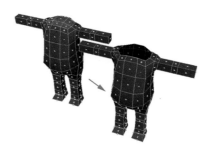

25 Now start working on the neck. Select the faces above the collar and delete them.

26 Select the edges around the opening and extrude them. Scale them down and flatten them in the vertical direction so they make a nice oval that will act as the base of the neck.

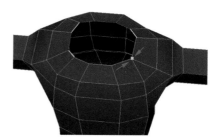

27 In order for this detail to match up with the head, we need to reduce the opening from 12 vertices to 8. Select the edges at each of the four corners and collapse them. This will reduce the vertex count.

28 Select the edges around the neck opening, and extrude them twice to create the neck. We will attach it to the head later.

31 Extrude the polygon representing the base of the thumb several times to make the thumb.

34 Extrude the face at the base of the palm several times to create the base of the glove and sculpt it into shape.

29 The body is done. Touch up any rough spots and refine it until you're happy.

32 Select the faces at the front of the palm. Extrude them, making sure the Keep Faces Together attribute is toggled off. This will create the fingers.

35 The hand is done. Although it might look blocky, it will subdivide nicely. You can test to see how the hand will subdivide by choosing Modify → Convert → Polygons To Subdiv.

30 Here we begin modeling the glove. The hand starts with a simple box approximately the size of the character's palm. The box should have three subdivisions each of width and depth.

33 The basic topology of the hand is now in place. Resculpt the vertices to get a more natural shape.

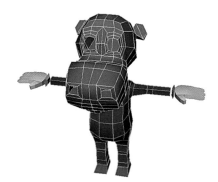

Now that all the parts are built, we need to bring them together as one character. The first step is to get all the parts in one scene and then scale and align all the parts of the character.

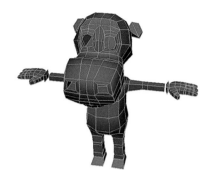

1 Select all the parts of the character, and then choose Mesh → Combine to combine all the parts into the same object.

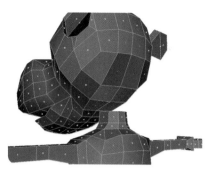

4 You attach the head in much the same way as you attached the hands. Select the four polygons that represent the base of the skull and delete them.

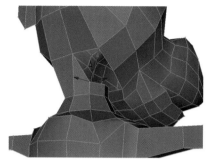

5 Snap the vertices of the top of the neck to the corresponding vertices of the head. Choose Edit Mesh → Merge to seamlessly connect the head to the body.

2 Attach the gloves at the wrists. First, delete the faces that are at the ends of the arm and the hand.

3 Snap the vertices of the end of the arm to the corresponding vertices of the glove. Choose Edit Mesh → Merge to make the joints seamless. Repeat the process on the other hand.

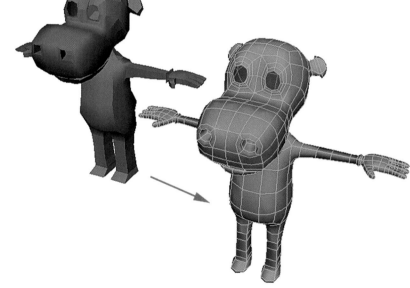

6 The model is finished. Create a subdivision surface of the model by choosing Modify → Convert → Polygons To Subdiv.

Modeling a Mug Using Subdiv Proxy

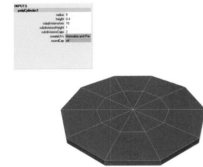

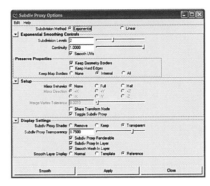

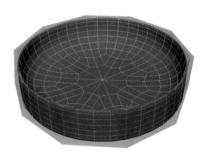

1 We'll start the model from a simple cylinder polygon primitive. Choose Create → Polygon Primitives → Cylinder.

2 In the Inputs section of the Channel box, click on the cylinder's object name to expand its cylinder input channels (alternatively, you can open the Attribute Editor and edit the cylinder's attributes there). Change Radius to 5, Height to 0.4, Subdivisions Axis to 10, Subdivisions Height to 1, and Subdivisions Caps to 2. This will set us up for the base of the mug.

3 We will now convert the model into Subdiv Proxy. Choose Proxy → Subdiv Proxy ❑. Match your settings to this screenshot; this will subdivide the smooth version twice and make the proxy model transparent but still modifiable. The idea is to edit the low-res proxy while constantly viewing the subdivided high-res version.

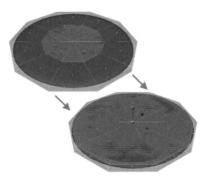

4 Select the top-middle faces of the low-res model (all editing in this tutorial will be on this proxy). Scale the faces out so that the top-outer faces are thin; these outer faces represent the thickness of the mug.

5 Select the top-outer faces. Choose Edit Mesh → Extrude, and translate the new extruded faces upward. This will be the starting point for the sides of the mug.

6 Continue to extrude up the sides and shape the curvature of the mug. Six vertical segments should suffice.

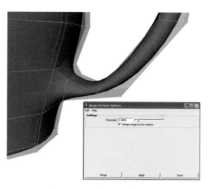

7 Next, select an outer face toward the top of the mug. Extrude the face and scale the extruded face inward to begin the base of the handle.

10 Next, we'll need to join the handle to the bottom part of the mug by merging the vertices from the handle to the vertices you extruded in the previous step. Select the eight vertices and choose Edit Mesh → Merge ❑. A threshold of 1 should suffice for this example. The handle should now be connected to the lower part of the mug by four merged vertices.

11 We'll add some creasing and sharpness to the handle. Select the two outer edges of the handle and choose Proxy → Crease Proxy Edge Tool. MMB-drag to the right to increase the intensity of the crease.

8 Continue extruding and shaping the handle. Work its shape down so that it ends up near a face toward the bottom of the mug.

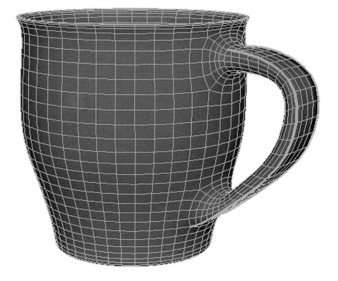

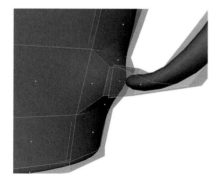

9 As you did in step 7, extrude a face toward the bottom of the mug in order to connect the handle. Select the extruded face and delete it. Also, delete the connecting face of the handle.

12 Tweak the proxy mesh as you wish to get the mug shape you want. Finally, turn off the visibility of the proxy display layer to see the smoothed version of the mug.

Modeling a Boat Using Subdivision Surfaces

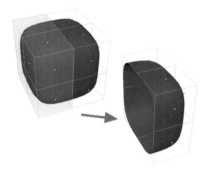

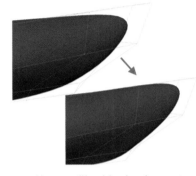

1 We'll start the model from a simple subdivision cube primitive. Choose Create → Subdiv Primitives → Cube. By default, the display smoothness is 1. Press the 3 key to display the cube at its smoothest.

3 Select all the faces on the left side of the cube and delete them. Since the boat will be symmetrical, we'll model a lot of the detail on one side and then mirror it later. Try not to break the line of symmetry when doing any of the following sculpting.

5 Next we'll add edge loops to the front and rear of the boat to help give shape. Choose Edit Mesh → Insert Edge Loop Tool. Click-drag anywhere toward the back end of the boat and add a vertical edge loop. Add another edge loop toward the front end of the boat.

2 Right-click over the cube to bring up the Sub-d marking menu and choose Polygon to enter polygon editing mode. We can now edit the model's components as if they were polygons.

4 Begin molding the basic shape of the boat by pulling vertices. For mirroring reasons, try not to move the inside-edge vertices away from the line of symmetry.

6 The new edge loops allow you to refine the shape of the boat's hull. Move the new vertices to better define the boat shape.

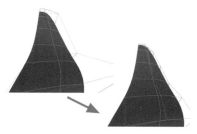

7 Next, we'll begin the boat's cavity. Right-click over the boat to bring up the Sub-d marking menu and choose Standard to return to standard editing mode. Select the two faces on the top of the boat. Choose Subdiv Surfaces → Refine Selected Components. The selected faces and their neighbors will subdivide to give you more detail.

10 While still in standard editing mode, select the edges around the cavity. To make the edges around the cavity a bit harder, choose Subdiv Surfaces → Partial Crease Edge/Vertex. Do this twice.

12 Delete the history on the mirrored half by selecting it and choosing Edit → Delete By Type → History. Then select both halves and choose Subdiv Surfaces → Attach. You may want to uncheck Keep Originals in the attach options.

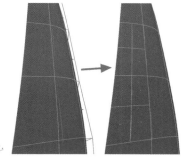

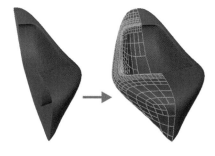

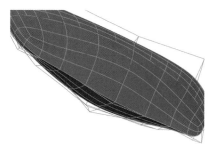

8 Select the two top-middle faces and refine them. This will give us a bit more detail for modeling the cavity.

11 Check to be sure that all of the inner vertices of the boat half are planar (rather, they all lie exactly on the same plane). This is crucial for mirroring to work properly! Select the boat and choose Subdiv Surfaces → Mirror ❑. In the mirror options, choose the axis you want to mirror about (in this illustrated example, the X axis). Press the Apply button.

13 Next select the edges along the bottom of the boat. Since we want a very crisp and hard edge here, choose Subdiv Surfaces → Full Crease Edge/Vertex.

9 Move and scale the new faces to shape out the boat's cavity. Remember to not to break the line of symmetry when doing this, so that we can correctly mirror the geometry later.

14 As a final touch, create a few sub-d cubes, and then scale and position them within the cavity.

15 Now that the boat is done, we'll start on the oars. Start by creating a sub-d cube.

16 Go to polygon editing mode. Select the top four faces of the cube.

17 Choose Edit Mesh → Extrude and translate the extruded faces upward.

18 Scale the extruded faces out to start the bottom half of the oar head.

19 Extrude the top faces again, and then scale and position them to round out the top of the head.

20 To anticipate the round shape of the handle, shape the vertices at the bottom in a circular fashion.

21 Extrude the bottom four faces down twice to create the oar handle.

22 To cap off the bottom of the oar, extrude the faces one last time. Doing this will prevent tapering.

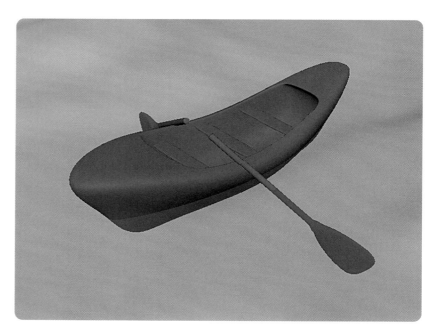

Creating Textures

T
extures bring a model and a scene to life. Without texture, most 3D models would look like solid plastic when rendered. Textures bring color, reflections, transparency, and roughness to a surface. You can create textures from images such as photographs or paintings, and you can also create them procedurally using texture generators that come with Maya.

You create textures in Maya using Shader networks, which are networks of interconnected nodes. Understanding how these nodes work and how they affect surface characteristics is important to mastering texturing within Maya. Getting a texture right can take a lot of revisions. In the production process, many times you create textures along with the lighting, as light has direct bearing on how a surface will look. Using tools such as Maya's Interactive Photorealistic Rendering (IPR) can also help fine-tune textures much more quickly.

Shaders

In Maya, shaders control the way a surface looks. Attributes such as transparency, reflectivity, bumps, color, and texture are all contained within a shader. Shaders in Maya are actually constructed from a network of nodes. Each node contains attributes that define the way the shader behaves, such as the color or transparency of the shader.

When creating a shader, first you need to decide the type of surface you will be shading. Different types of surfaces react differently to light. Maya has five basic shading types, also known as surface materials. Each shader type deals with light uniquely, particularly when handling specularity or how shiny an object appears.

Lambert: Creates a diffuse surface with no highlights. Perfect for any type of nonreflective surface, such as rubber or cloth.

Phong: One of the oldest shading algorithms and creates a surface with distinct specular highlights. Supports reflections and is good for creating shiny artificial surfaces such as plastics and some glass.

Phong E: Similar to Phong but with additional attributes that allow for greater control and softer highlights. Good for glass or any shiny organic surface.

Blinn: A versatile shading algorithm and probably the most popular among artists. Has fairly soft highlights by default, but can simulate almost anything from a Lambert to a Phong. Used for almost anything from skin to metal.

Anisotropic: Simulates surfaces that have directional highlights. Good for such materials as brushed metal, silk, and hair.

Ramp Shader

A Ramp shader can simulate the way color changes with changing light and the view angle. It's great for surfaces such as silk and satin, but can also tweak traditional shading in subtle ways as well as produce effects such as x-ray shading.

 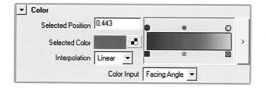

When the Color attribute of the Ramp shader is mapped to change according to viewing angle, the color of the surface changes as the surface curves away. Even adding a subtle change in color truly brings a surface to life.

 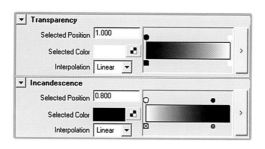

Applying a ramp to the Transparency and Incandescence attributes produces an x-ray effect.

Layered Shader

A layered shader allows multiple layers to be stacked and combined. It is useful for shading objects with multiple materials. You can composite layers in myriad ways using image maps, ramps, or mattes.

Creating and Editing Shaders

Maya allows you to create, edit, and manage shaders in several ways. You can create shaders from the Render shelf, the Multilister, or the Hypershade window. You can edit Shader networks using the Attributes panel of the shader or within the Hypershade window, and you can manage shaders with either the Multilister or the Hypershade window.

The Render shelf allows you to create and assign any type of shader to the active objects in the scene. Simply select the objects and RMB the desired shader. This is an easy way to quickly assign basic shader types to objects.

Shader Attributes

The most direct way to edit a shader's properties is through the shader's Attributes panel. Any object that has the shader applied has an Attributes panel for the shader. Since shaders can be shared among objects, modifying a single object's shader can affect other objects as well.

Name The name of the shader. Each shader should have a unique and descriptive name. One shader can be shared among many objects.

Material Sample A sample of what the shader will look like when rendered.

Material Type The type of surface material.

Common Material Attributes The attributes shared by every shader, which include color, transparency, and bump mapping, among others.

Specular Shading Since each surface material type handles specularity differently, these parameters depend on the type of shader.

Common Attributes

The first group of attributes is common to all Maya shader types. These attributes define the color, transparency, and bumpiness of the surface. All shader attributes are nodes that can contain a simple value, such as an RGB color or a grayscale value. Nodes can also be connected to other nodes, such as a texture, for creating more-complex shaders.

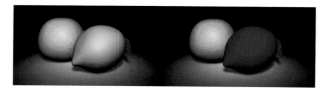

Color: An RGB value (here, yellow vs. blue) defined by the color wheel. The color can also be defined by a texture node that contains a bitmap or a procedural texture.

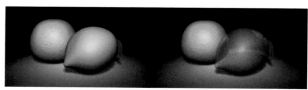

Transparency: Usually defined by a grayscale bitmap, but can also contain color. (Here, Transparency is set as left 0.0, right 0.5.) Color transparencies might be used in a stained-glass window, for example.

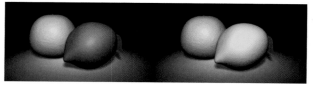

Ambient Color: The overall color of the object in the absence of light. (Ambient left 0.5, right 0.9.) Increasing this value can give the illusion of ambient lighting in a well-lit scene, but if the scene goes dark, too much ambient color makes the object appear lighter than the background.

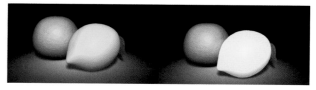

Incandescence: For objects that are self-illuminated, such as light fixtures. This attribute does not emit light, however, and will not light other objects. (Incandescence left 0.3, right 0.7.) Turning this up makes the object appear more of a solid color.

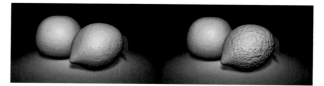

Bump Mapping: Creates the illusion of surface relief by simulating the highlights and shadows caused by a bumpy surface. (Bump left 0.4, right 0.8.) This attribute requires a texture node, such as a bitmap or noise node. Bump mapping is simulated and does not actually change the surface, simply the way light bounces off it. (Displacement maps change the surface.)

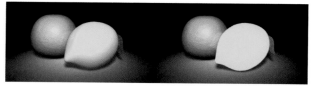

Diffuse: Determines how much light is absorbed or scattered by the surface. (Diffuse left 0.5, right 1.0.) This value determines the overall brightness of the object when it is illuminated by a light.

Translucence, Depth, and Focus: Allows the surface to transmit light diffusely, like frosted glass, wax, leaves, or clouds. Higher Translucence transmits more light; Translucence Focus determines how much light is scattered. A surface's translucence is based on the illumination it receives from lights and is not related to its transparency.

Specular Attributes

Specularity determines how shiny an object appears, and the eye uses specularity to determine the quality and character of a surface. The attributes controlling specularity depend on the shader's surface material. Lambert shaders, for example, have no specular attributes; Blinn, Phong, and Anisotropic shaders each have their own ways of creating specular highlights.

(left) An object without specularity appears to have a matte finish. (right) Specularity adds highlights to the object and gives it shininess.

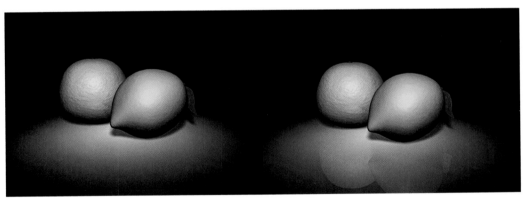

Reflectivity is also configured in the Specular Shading rollout tab. An object's reflectivity determines how much the object reflects its environment, determined by either the reflected color or actual raytracing.

Connecting Textures to Attributes

The easiest way to add texture maps to an attribute is to apply them within the Attributes panel. Any mappable attribute has a little checkered box along the right side of its controls. Clicking this box allows you to choose a texture type.

TIP Clicking the checkered icon to the right of an attribute opens the Create Render Node window. The Create Render Node window allows you to choose a type of render node, such as a texture, and connect it to the attribute.

The Hypershade

The Hypershade window (choose Window → Rendering Editors → Hypershade) is the preferred place to create and edit shaders, as well as manage textures, lights, and special effects. The Hypershade window displays shaders as connected nodes, much in the same way as the Hypergraph window, allowing you to edit shaders by connecting and disconnecting nodes to create Shader networks.

Graphing icons Allow you to graph and display a Shader network in the work area. You can also access these functions under the Graph menu in the Hypershade.

Connections Allow you to view the input and/or output connections to a node in the network. Handy for viewing small sections of a complex network. You can also access these functions under the Graph menu in the Hypershade.

Hypershade tabs Provide a tabbed interface to organize your projects. By default, materials, textures, lights, and cameras all have their own tabs. You can create additional tabs using the Tabs option in the Hypershade menu.

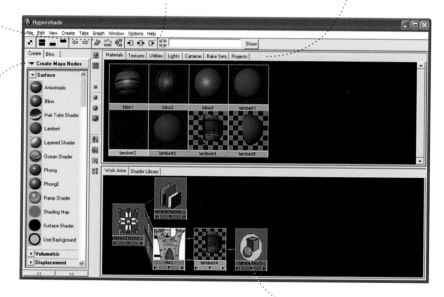

Create bar Use to create surface materials, textures, lights, displacements, environments, glows, and volumetric effects. These tabs also have utilities you can use to place textures, adjust color, and manage particles. You can also access these functions under the Create menu in the Hypershade.

Work area Where Shader networks can be edited. Navigation is the same as in any viewport. Moving the mouse over a connection displays the type of connection. MMB and dragging one node over another creates a connection.

> **TIP**　Using the Multilister window (choose Window → Rendering Editors → Multilister) is another way to manage and create textures and has been around since Alias PowerAnimator. It is a simpler interface than the Hypershade window, and for basic textures, it can be a faster way to manage texture libraries. The Multilister window has two panes: on the top is a tabbed interface containing all the Shader networks, materials, lights, and cameras in the scene; along the bottom are textures associated with the scene.

Using the Hypershade

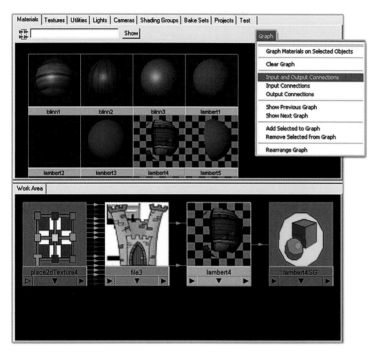

Nodes are created using the Create Maya Nodes panel. When creating a shader, you start with the surface material type. You can also create textures, such as this file being used as a texture map.

Modifying a Shader network requires that you graph it. This is done using the window's menu or the marking menu or by clicking the Connections button on the toolbar. The graph of the network appears in the work area.

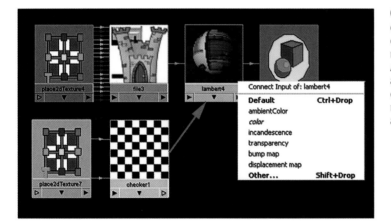

Connections between nodes can be made simply by MM clicking and dragging the node over the desired target. A short list of attributes appears, allowing you to connect the output of the node to the most common attributes.

TIP   If a node is not listed in the shortcut menu, choose Other and use the Connection Editor to make the connection.

Textures

Textures are images that can be mapped to almost any attribute of a surface material. Color is the most common type of texture; a wood table might use a digital image of wood grain as its color attribute, for example. Textures can also be used for many other attributes, such as bump mapping, transparency, and reflectivity.

Textures can be bitmap images or can be created procedurally. Bitmaps can be any sort of image, from a product logo to a digital photograph, but large textures can consume a lot of disk space and system memory. Procedural textures use mathematical algorithms to create patterns, such as noise, gradients, and checkerboards, and can be much more efficient than bitmaps. Since they are generated mathematically, they don't take up disk space and are resolution independent. Procedural textures fall into two categories, 2D and 3D; 3D textures create texture information in a third dimension and must be mapped differently.

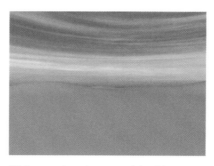

Without color, the ground in this scene has no character.

In this case, a photograph of some dirt and asphalt is used to add some color.

Another bitmap texture is used to map the bumpiness of the surface.

The final result has much more character.

Bitmapped Textures

Creating bitmap textures is often done in image-editing applications such as Photoshop. The big thing to consider when creating a bitmap texture is the size of the bitmap. The bitmap needs to have enough resolution so that it doesn't break up when it is rendered. This resolution can be tricky to figure out, as a bitmap for an object in the background requires far less resolution than an object that is full screen.

(left) When the camera is above the ground, the textures look sharp and clear. (right) If the camera gets too close to the ground, however, the bitmap breaks up, causing a blurred effect. To fix this, you need a higher-resolution bitmap.

Creating Bitmapped Textures Using 3D Paint

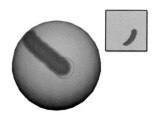

Maya offers the basic, but functional, 3D Paint tool (choose Texturing → 3D Paint Tool in the Rendering menu set) that allows you to create bitmapped textures by painting directly on a 3D model.

Before you can begin painting, the model needs texture coordinates applied. The default UV mapping can be used for NURBS models, though multiple patch models need multiple texture maps. A polygonal model typically uses a single texture map, necessitating a higher-resolution map. If the resolution gets too high, the model can be broken into multiple textures, one each for the head, body, and so on.

When you paint on a model, the paint is stored in a bitmap texture that has been assigned to the model. You can create and assign this texture directly from the 3D Paint tool. You can also paint over existing textures previously assigned in the Hypershade or through the shader's Attributes panel. When the tool is selected, an Artisan brush appears above the model.

Standard Charcoal Frost

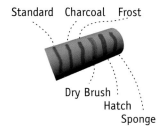

Dry Brush
Hatch
Sponge

The size and shape of the 3D Paint tool are determined using the U and L sliders. To choose the type of brush, click an icon below the U and L sliders. Brushes are pressure sensitive. To load a custom brush, click the Browse button.

Different brush types pro-duce different effects.

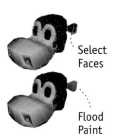

Select Faces

Flood Paint

The color of the brush. Reducing opacity allows you to paint over another color without entirely replacing it.

Flood Paint allows you to flood an entire area with a color. Flood Erase removes color, revealing the original texture.

3D painting on polygonal and subdivision surfaces allows you to flood selected faces. Simply select the faces, activate the 3D Paint tool, and toggle Selected before flooding.

Allows the brush to paint color, as well as erase, smear, clone, or blur. Set Erase Image is typically used to define the original image used to erase paint, but it can be any image, so you can use it to paint patterns.

This is where you define the attribute to paint, as well as the image format of the painted image. Images are stored in the 3DPaintTextures folder of the current project. This panel also allows you to save bitmaps or set the tool to save as you paint. (For large files, this can impact performance.)

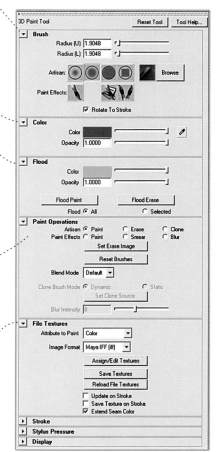

2D Procedural Textures

2D procedural textures operate much like bitmaps. You can map them to any object using UV coordinates, and you can also tile them. Procedural textures can be useful because they can quickly create natural-looking effects quickly and with little overhead. You can also animate procedural textures by keyframing their attributes.

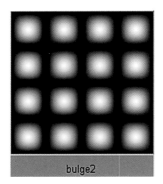

bulge2

checker2

cloth2

fractal1

Bulge: Creates a grid of white squares that fade to gray toward the edges.

Checker: Creates a two-color checkerboard pattern.

Cloth: Simulates woven fabric.

Fractal: Generates fractal noise and is often used to create natural phenomena.

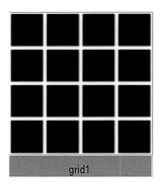

grid1

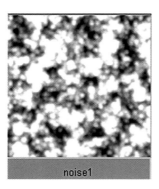

noise1

Color Key

Matte

Grid: Creates a grid pattern for simulating regular tiles and, as a transparency map, can create meshes.

Noise: Generates noise to simulate a bumpy surface or add variations in color.

Stencil: Used when applying a bitmap or procedural texture over a specific area of a model, such as when creating a label or a decal. Stencils can use a color key or a separate matte to mask out the desired area.

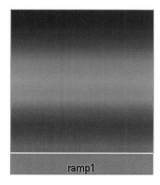

ramp1

Ramp: Gradients of two or more colors. These can be used as color maps to represent a sky and a horizon, flames, stripes, clouds, or patterns. They can also be used as mattes to blend between different textures or create a transparency.

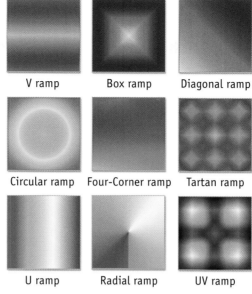

V ramp   Box ramp   Diagonal ramp

Circular ramp   Four-Corner ramp   Tartan ramp

U ramp   Radial ramp   UV ramp

Ramp types

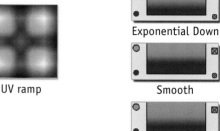

None

Linear

Exponential Up

Exponential Down

Smooth

Bump

Spike

Interpolation types

Ramp Attributes

Determines how the ramp will be calculated.

Determines how the colors will transition from one to the other. Choosing None creates hard-edged stripes.

Click the handle to choose color. Click and drag to choose position.

Opens the Color Chooser. Selecting Position moves the associated handle.

Type   V Ramp
Interpolation   Linear

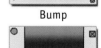

Selected Color
Selected Position   0.470
U Wave   0.000
V Wave   0.000
Noise   0.000
Noise Freq   0.500

Click inside the ramp to create a new handle and color.

Click to delete the handle and color.

Noise and Noise Freq introduce noise to the ramp.

U Wave and V Wave create a wavelike pattern along one or both axes of the ramp.

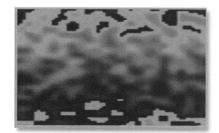

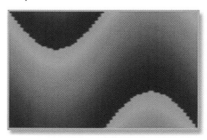

3D Procedural Textures

3D textures behave differently from 2D textures. A 2D texture is much like a sheet of paper that is laid on the surface. 3D textures, however, exist in a volume of 3D space, so the surface takes up the texture where it intersects with the volume.

brownian1

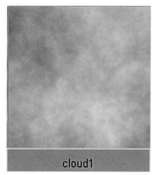

cloud1

leather1

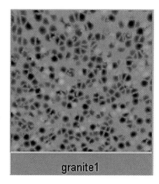

granite1

Brownian: A noisy texture based on the motion of particles in a liquid. When used as a bump map, Brownian is good for creating effects such as thickly painted metal.

Cloud: Creates clouds with transparent space in between. It's best to use it mapped onto a sphere to create a dome to represent the sky. You can use several spheres to create layered clouds.

Leather: Simulates the appearance of leather using two colors—one for the cell, and one for the veins between the cells. This can be quite effective for skin textures.

Granite: Gives the appearance of granite using a cell-like structure. This is the same as the Leather texture, except three cell colors are used instead of one. This makes it useful for skin textures in addition to simulating rock.

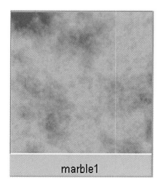

marble1

rock1

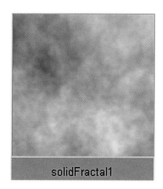

solidFractal1

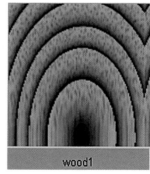

wood1

Marble: A veiny, pseudo-random texture that can simulate marble. It can be used for many other things, including clouds and lightning.

Rock: Simulates rock using a random 3D distribution of two grain material types.

Solid Fractal: Similar to the 2D Fractal, but this occupies a volume. It's great for volumetric effects such as clouds.

Wood: Simulates wood by creating concentric ring layers surrounded by veins and filler. Since this is a 3D texture, it simulates the veins of wood in 3D, which means that the veins are visible across corners and edges. This sort of effect is difficult using bitmaps.

Bump and Displacement Mapping

Bump maps give a surface a sense of roughness and depth. Most surfaces are not perfectly smooth, and a little bit of bump mapping can go a long way toward making objects seem real. It is also easier and more efficient to add surface imperfections using bump or displacement maps than to actually model every bump and pockmark on a surface.

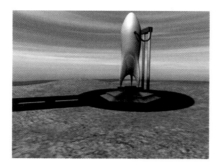

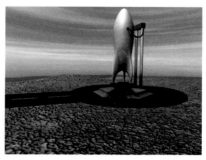

(left) With just a color map, the ground in this scene looks flat, fairly smooth, and not very convincing. (right) A bump map gives the ground a sense of roughness and adds an additional level of realism.

Bump Maps

Bump mapping can be configured within the material's Attributes panel. Bump mapping only affects the way light interacts with the surface, but does not actually modify geometry; so the edges still appear smooth. Bump mapping is perfectly fine for creating general surface roughness or more-exaggerated bumps on surfaces such as a ground plane or a wall.

Specularity is a good indicator of surface roughness. The highlight on this surface is smooth, making it look like a rubber ball. Adding a small amount of noise as a bump map turns the surface into the skin of an orange. This roughness shows up distinctly in the specular highlight.

Displacement Maps

Displacement mapping actually changes the surface of the geometry, adding another level of realism. This process takes significantly more processing and rendering power, so use displacements only where they are needed and use bumps for the rest. You can also use displacements as a modeling tool. Choose Modify → Convert → Displacement to Polygons, which generates a polygonal mesh.

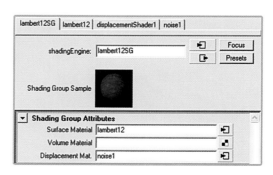

(left) A simple rock—no bumps or displacements. (center) With noise added as a bump map, the rock appears to have a rough surface. The edge of the rock, however, remains smooth. (right) A displacement map actually moves and changes the surface at render time to match the texture map. This completes the illusion.

To set up a displacement map, add it to the Displacement Mat attribute in the Shading Group (SG) tab in the shader's Attribute Editor.

Placing Textures

Proper placement of textures can be an important task. Many times, details of a texture need to line up precisely with details of the model. Placing a texture depends on the type of geometry as well as the type of texture.

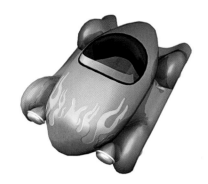

Mapping 2D Textures

In Maya, 2D textures are aligned using the place2dTexture node. This node is created automatically whenever a 2D texture is created. Nodes can also be shared, for times when you need to map similar textures along identical coordinates, such as a color and a transparency map.

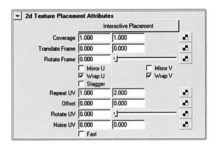

The 2d Texture Placement Attributes window contains attributes to control the placement of the texture.

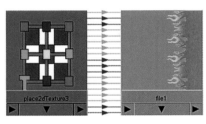

The place2dTexture node is automatically connected to the 2D texture when it is created. You can also connect this node to other textures so that many textures can share the same mapping.

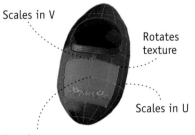

Scales in V
Rotates texture
Scales in U
Translates texture

Interactive Placement: Shows a manipulator that controls the way the texture is mapped to the surface. The manipulator has handles to scale, translate, and rotate the texture. Middle-clicking a handle adjusts the desired attribute.

Mapping 3D Textures

3D procedural textures, environment maps, and projected 2D textures need to be mapped to an object in three dimensions. This is done using the place3DTexture node, which creates a texture reference object in the scene. You can move, rotate, scale, and shear this object in both world and local space to place the texture correctly within the scene.

Projections on Polygons

Projecting an image on a surface is similar to how a slide projector works. The image is cast onto the object from a specific direction and angle. Textures can also be projected from spheres,

Texture projected on an object.

cubes, and cylinders, among other shapes, to essentially turn a 2D texture into a 3D texture.

Polygonal objects have projection options that can be applied through the Create UVs menu in the Polygons menu set. Simply select the polygonal mesh (or selected faces in the mesh) and choose Create UVs → Planar, Cylindrical, or Spherical Mapping. This applies the projection and provides a manipulator to adjust the placement.

Planar: Projects the texture along a plane. The positioning, size, and rotation of the plane can be adjusted with the manipulator.

Cylindrical: Wraps the texture into a cylindrical shell and projects it on the surface. The manipulator has options for size, position, and rotation, as well as sweep angle.

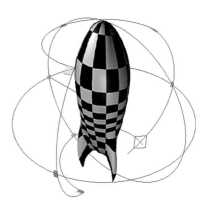

Spherical: Applies the texture to a spherical shell and projects it on the surface. The manipulator has options for size, position, and rotation, as well as sweep angle.

UV Texture Editing

One of the big benefits of polygonal modeling is that polygonal objects are not limited to patches or networks of patches. Polygonal objects can have branches and multiple surfaces. This, however, makes it difficult to texture them with simple projections or 2D image placement.

Using Maya's UV Texture Editor (choose Window → UV Texture Editor) is the best way to edit the texture mapping on a complex polygonal object. It allows you to lay a wireframe representation of the object against a texture map and place textures exactly by adjusting the positions of the object's UV coordinates.

A complex mesh containing multiple mapping coordinates and projections. This can be accomplished using the UV Texture Editor.

The texture map contains images for all parts of the object.

The process of mapping starts by creating a basic set of UV coordinates for the object. Selecting faces of the object and projecting mapping coordinates on the sets of faces is one way to apply UV coordinates. Another way is to use automatic mapping (choose Create UVs → Automatic Mapping).

Once the basic UV mapping is applied, you can use the UV Texture Editor to fine-tune and adjust the mapping. By setting the component mode to UV, you can move, separate, and sew the object's UV coordinates to other parts of the model.

Flip and rotate UVs These four icons allow you to flip sets of UVs along an axis or rotate them 45° at a time.

Sew and split UVs Icons that allow you to sew UVs together for seamless texturing, as well as split UVs into individual sets so they can be positioned independently.

UV space tools Tools that change the arrangement of the UVs within the UV space.

Align UVs Tools that let you align, snap, and relax sets of UVs.

Isolation tools Many times, UVs can overlap, making selection and tweaking difficult. These tools allow you to isolate sets of UVs while hiding the rest, making editing easier.

View buttons Icons that allow you to control the way images and grids appear in the Texture View pane.

UV Modification Tools Tools that let you move UVs in various ways.

UVs Selected UVs are highlighted in green.

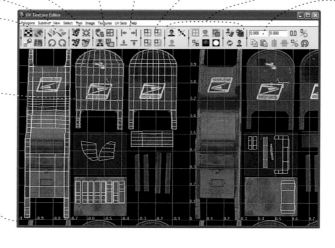

UV edit buttons Tools that allow you to cut and paste UVs.

Texture view Where UV texture editing takes place. Navigate in the way you navigate any other orthogonal viewport. You can select and move UVs using the standard Move, Rotate, and Scale tools. In addition, you can separate or sew UVs together.

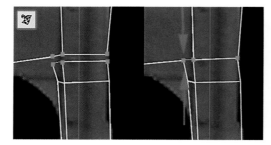

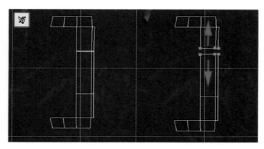

To sew UVs together, select the UVs and then click the Sew UVs button (choose Polygons → Sew UV Edges). This connects the selected UVs to match the topology of the model. Move and Sew UV Edges moves an entire UV set to match another and automatically sews the two together.

To split UVs, select the desired edges and then click the Split UVs button (choose Polygons → Cut UV Edges). This disconnects the UVs around the selected edges. You can also split UVs at a specific UV by clicking the Split Selected UV button.

Reflection Mapping

Any shiny object reflects light. Reflections are important in simulating reality. A mirror might reflect an image perfectly, while galvanized metal might only reflect broad swaths of color, but they both reflect at least a little bit of their environment.

The most accurate form of reflections come from raytracing, but many artists simply use bitmapped environments. Although not as accurate, bitmapped environments can be much faster to render, and, in most cases, reflections do not need to be completely accurate to sell the illusion of reality. If there is no "real" environment, such as when an object is rendered by itself, bitmap environments are a necessity. They are particularly useful when creating animation that integrates with film or video. Artists who work on special effects often take photographs of the film sets in order to generate bitmap reflections.

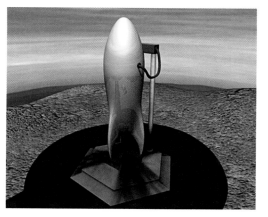

This rocket appears to be made of chrome because it reflects its environment. These particular reflections were created using raytracing, so actual objects within the environment, such as the road, are reflected on the rocket's surface.

Raytracing is set up in the shader's attributes under raytracing. Raytracing must also be turned on in the Render Settings window.

Raytraced reflections do not need mapping, as the reflection is generated directly from the objects in the scene. The reflectivity attribute of the material determines the amount of light the surface reflects.

Setting up mapped reflections takes a few more steps, but they are quicker to render and more flexible when rendering objects individually rather than with an entire scene.

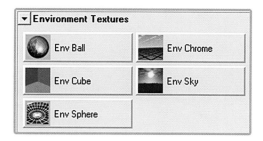

Mapped reflections are set up using environment maps. There are several procedural maps, plus some tools to assist in mapping bitmaps as environmental reflections.

Environment Sky is a procedural texture that creates a sky, clouds, a sun, and a ground plane. It is best used for outdoor scenes.

Environment Chrome simulates an indoor scene, with a floor, a roof, and grids to represent floor tiles and lights.

Environment Sphere, Ball, and Cube are mapping types that project an image to be used as a reflection. This is useful when you have a real-world reference from the scene.

Photoshop Integration

Although Adobe Photoshop is a separate graphics package from Adobe, Maya supports the Photoshop PSD format. PSD files save their image data on user-defined layers. These layers within a single PSD file can be used to encapsulate multiple textures to be used in a material. Furthermore, Maya supports image output to the Photoshop format, in order to make postproduction work easier.

A Photoshop network can be created on an object by choosing Texturing → Create PSD Network. When you create a network, specify which attributes you wish to include within the file. Since textures often are drawn on a UV map, you can include a snapshot of the UVs within their own layer.

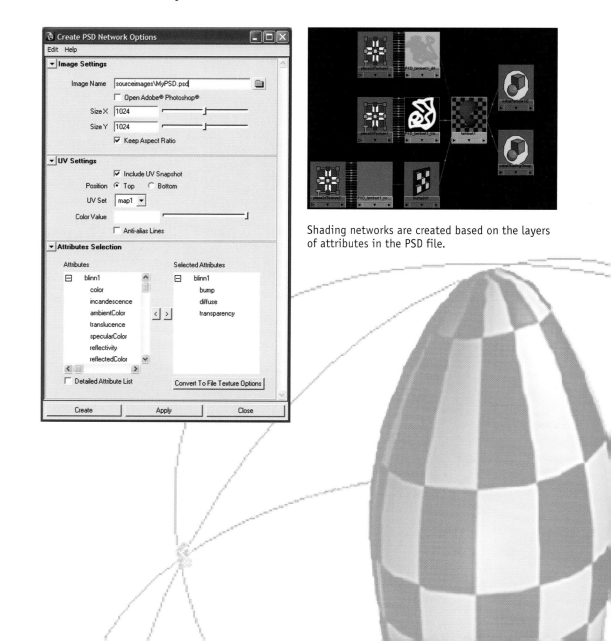

Shading networks are created based on the layers of attributes in the PSD file.

Updating a PSD

After you have edited a Maya-exported PSD within Photoshop, simply save the Photoshop file and then in Maya choose Texturing → Update PSD Networks. Any changes you have made within the Photoshop layers will update the shading network.

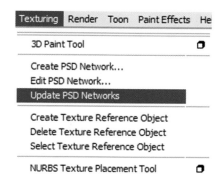

Rendering to Photoshop Format

Render layers are used for rendering the scene in multiple passes. You can specify the image format in the Render Settings as PSD Layered, so that each render layer corresponds to a Photoshop layer. Rendering images in this way allows for easier postproduction work, and is great for consolidating multiple render passes into a single file.

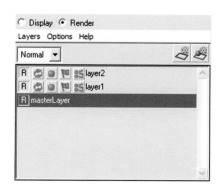

Render layers can be used to create separate images for different objects.

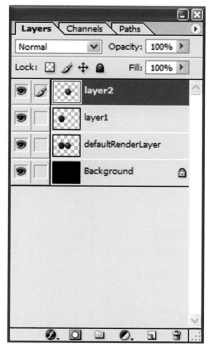

When opened in Photoshop, the layers directly correspond to the render layers created in Maya.

Mapping a Car Using Multiple Textures

1 Open the scene Ch04_Car_start.mb, which contains the car. If you want, you can use the car you built in Chapter 2.

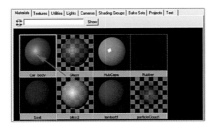

2 Open the Hypershade window. Select the Car_body shader, which provides color for the car, fenders, and headlight shells. We want to add texture to only the body, so we need to create a new shader.

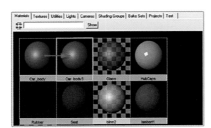

3 Choose Edit → Duplicate → Shading Network to duplicate the entire shader.

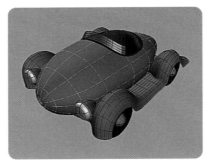

4 Select the body of the car. In the Hypershade window, select the new shader and RMB it to open a marking menu. Choose Assign Material To Selection to apply this to the car body.

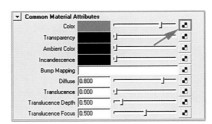

5 Let's add this map for the car's number to the color channel. Select the shader and press Ctrl+A/ ⌘+A to open the Common Material Attributes window.

6 In the Attributes Editor, click the checkered box next to the shader's Color attribute to open the Create Render Node window.

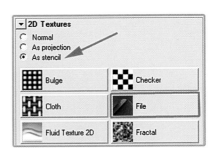

7 Since this texture is not square, we will need to use a stencil node to trim off the blue areas. Toggle the As Stencil button, and then choose File.

8 In the Attribute Editor, under the File tab, load the file Ch04_CarDecal.tga into the Image Name slot by clicking to the right of the slot and browsing the disk for the file.

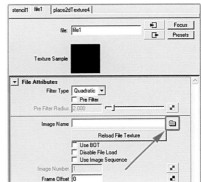

9 Look at the shading network in the Hypershade. The texture is connected to the stencil node, which is then connected to the material node.

10 Look at the texture in a viewport or do a test render. The decal is mapped on the car, but it is mapped way too large.

11 In the Hypershade window, select the place2dTexture node connected directly to the decal texture. In the Attribute Editor, use interactive placement to adjust the positioning of the texture or type the numbers directly: Coverage 0.16 in both U and V, Translate 0.475 in U and −0.063 in V, and Rotation of 180°.

12 Many graphics cards will not display the decal perfectly, so a test render can ensure it is mapped properly. We now need to mask out the blue areas of the decal.

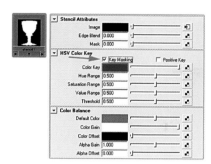

13 In the Hypershade, select the stencil node. In the Common Material Attributes window, under HSV Color Key, toggle Key Masking and set Color Key to pure blue (0, 0, 255).

14 Another test render shows the blue areas have been masked out. The rest of the car is gray, however, and we need to fix that with another map.

15 Go to the Create panel in the Hypershade window. Under the 2D Textures tab, select File. Since this texture will not need to be stenciled, toggle Normal before creating the node.

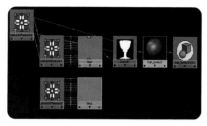

16 This will create a blank texture node in the shader's work area, along with a place2dTexture node. Select the blank texture node, and go to the Common Material Attributes window.

17 Load the file Ch04_CarFlames.tga into the node.

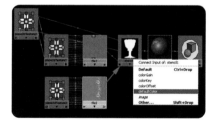

18 We need to connect this node so that it shows up in the shading network. In the Hypershade, select the new texture node, middle-click, and drag to the stencil node. A small menu will appear. Connect the attribute to Default-Color.

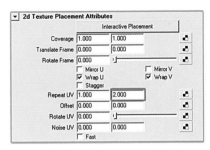

19 A test render shows that the color of the second map does show through, but only within the texture frame defined by the decal's mapping coordinates. The gray area is the default color of the decal's texture node.

21 A test render shows that the flame texture now covers the car. Last, we simply need to adjust the mapping of the flames to make them symmetrical.

22 Using the attributes of the flame texture's place2dTexture node, adjust the mapping so that it repeats 2.0 times in the V direction.

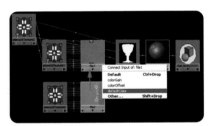

20 Middle-click and drag the flame texture over the decal texture. When the menu appears, select DefaultColor. This maps the flame texture into the gray area on the rest of the car.

23 Do a final test render. The car is complete.

5

Lighting

Any photographer can tell how important lighting is when taking a photograph. In the basic sense, photography is nothing more than capturing and recording light. Artists working in Maya also use light, but because it's a computer representation of light, there are subtle differences. Light, for example, may not bounce through a Maya scene exactly the way real-world lights would, but Maya provides a lot of features Mother Nature can't provide. In Maya, you can switch shadows on or off, sculpt light to change color over distance or stop dead in its tracks, and configure lights to hit an object but not its neighbor. Maya's wide array of tools allows for a very realistic simulation of the natural world but can also be used to create your own realities.

The Importance of Lighting

Proper lighting is one of the foundations of making good images. The color, character, and amount of light give your audience plenty of information about your images. Light tells people the difference between day and night or lets them know if something is scary, moody, or friendly. Light also helps define the form and shape of an object. Good lighting makes a good model look great, while poor lighting can make the best models look average.

A simple stage set with one light. The lighting in this scene is flat and does not do much to sell the image to the audience.

By adding a few spotlights, some color, and a projector for the backdrop, we can bring the stage to life.

Changing the lighting can quickly change the mood and tone of the scene, even from day to night.

Light can also be used to highlight the form of an object. When lit with one light, the car is acceptable, but not interesting.

When a few more lights are added, the form of the car is much more apparent and it comes to life.

Types of Lights

The various types of lighting can be accessed by choosing Create → Lights or by selecting them from the Render shelf. The default Maya renderer uses lights that can illuminate only what the light strikes. This can be a little counterintuitive; real objects tend to reflect and scatter secondary light. A white card next to an object in the real world, for example, reflects diffuse light onto the object. When using the Maya renderer, this type of secondary lighting must be simulated with a second light to represent the card.

Maya's mental ray renderer can do such real-world simulations. In mental ray, light can also come from Global Illumination (GI) sources. Global Illumination simulates the bouncing of light throughout a room. This creates a much more natural lighting, but at a significant increase in render time.

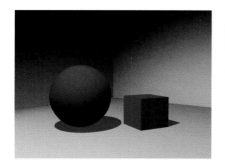

Standard lights in Maya do not bounce, so the undersides of these objects are nearly black because they do not receive light from the one light in the scene.

When Global Illumination is used in Maya's mental ray renderer, the exact same scene simulates the way light bounces around the room, turning the surfaces of the room into secondary light sources and creating a softer and more natural effect.

Regardless of how the renderer calculates secondary lighting, the basics of lighting in Maya are the same. All lights share three attributes: color, intensity, and illumination. Different types of lights also share other common attributes.

The color the light radiates, either a solid color or a texture map that can simulate gels, slides, or any other type of lighting setup.

A multiplier that scales the color by the intensity value. Intensity can also be a negative number that, in effect, removes light from the scene. Negative light intensities can be useful in adding darkness to a scene.

Used in conjunction with light linking. When toggled off, the light illuminates only specified objects.

Diffuse lighting illuminates the scene; specular illuminates the highlights. By toggling these, you can create custom lights that can create only specular highlights, allowing for finer control of highlight placement.

Determines the way the light decays over distance. Options include linear, quadratic, and cubic.

Used in spotlights; controls the spread of the light.

Used in spotlights; controls the softness of the edge of the light.

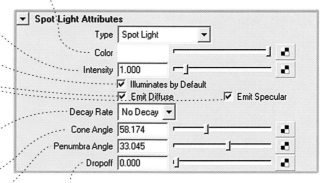

Used in spotlights; controls how the light fades from the center of the spot to the edge.

Ambient light is the simplest type of lighting in Maya. Ambient lights illuminate the entire scene fairly equally and don't cast shadows (unless raytracing is turned on). It's best to use ambient lights subtly to add an overall tone to a scene or to simulate bounced lighting. Generally, ambient lights tend to flatten a scene, but the Ambient Shade attribute allows Maya's ambient lights to act more like a point source to add shading without specularity.

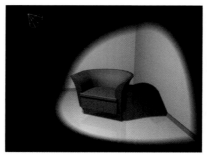

Spotlights originate from a single point and spread outward in a conical shape. Rotating them aims the light to illuminate specific spots of the scene. Spotlights can illuminate both diffuse and specular areas of a scene. They also can cast shadows and decay over distance. Cone Angle adjusts the size of the entire light, Penumbra controls the softness of the edge of the light cone, and Dropoff controls how quickly the light fades from the center to the edge.

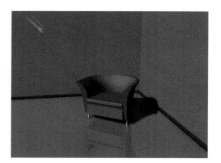

Directional lights are similar to spotlights in that they have a specific direction, but a directional light does not emanate from a single point. Instead, the rays are parallel and simulate distant lights such as the sun. This makes them ideal for outdoor scenes, but they do have limitations in that directional lights cannot decay or use effects such as fog or glow.

Point lights can be thought of as bare lightbulbs in the room. Like a lightbulb, a point light sends its rays in every direction. Similar to spotlights, point lights affect the specularity of an object and can cast shadows. The best use for a point light is as an overall scene light.

Area lights cast their light from an area, rather than from a point. This makes them a good choice for simulating diffuse lighting, bounce lights, or fluorescent tubes. When an area light is scaled, its intensity increases. Although area lights can provide realistic effects, calculating complex shadows can eat up a lot of render time.

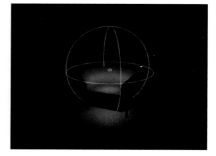

Volume lights are a special type of light that illuminate a specific volume, such as a sphere, a cone, or a cube. A major advantage of using a volume light is that you can limit light to a specific area of the scene. You can achieve different effects with light direction. Volume lights have several options. Outward behaves like a point light. Down Axis acts like a directional light. Inward reverses the light direction for shading, giving the appearance of inward illumination. Volume lights also have gradients to control the character of the light within the volume.

mental ray Lights

Directional, point, and spotlights in Maya can be used with the mental ray for Maya renderer, and most Maya lighting parameters translate with no effort. Each light has an Attributes panel for the mental ray options.

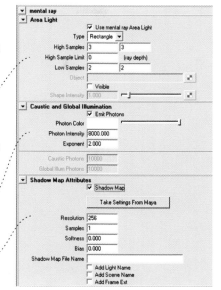

This panel allows you to create an area light that renders properly in mental ray. In addition to rectangular area lights, mental ray gives you several other shapes, including a disc, a sphere, a cylinder, or a custom shape that can be derived from another object.

Settings to control the emission of photons when used with Global Illumination in mental ray.

Normally, mental ray takes the shadow map information from the Maya light panel. This panel allows you to control the settings manually.

In addition to these lights, Maya includes a light type called mental ray IBL (Image Based Lighting). This is used to generate light from an image, such as an image of the sky, to create naturalistic lighting.

Adjusting Lights

Lights can be manipulated using the Attributes panel or the Channel box. The Show Manipulator tool allows you to adjust many of these parameters interactively.

The tool has several options, which are accessed by toggling the cycle index icon. These options include the ability to set the position of the light and its target location and adjust the cone angle, penumbra, and decay regions, among others.

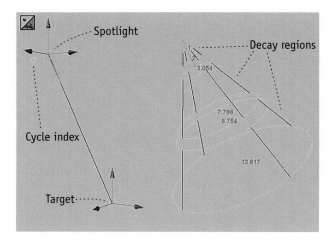

Adjusting light parameters using the Show Manipulator tool

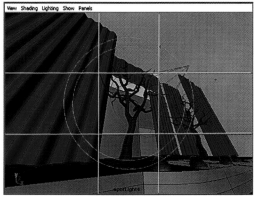

Another way to adjust lights is to look through them, much like a camera. Simply select the light and choose Look Through Selected to see the scene from the light's view. You can use camera navigation tools to position the light.

Shadows

Almost all objects cast shadows, and creating realistic shadows is one of the keys to truly simulating reality in Maya. Shadows add not only realism, but contribute greatly to the mood of a scene; they help the eye determine the placement of objects in a scene, and they visually anchor objects to the ground.

Shadows add to the realism of the scene and help anchor objects to the ground.

Raytraced shadows (right) render shadows through transparent objects, but depth map shadows (left) won't.

Depth Map Shadows

Depth map shadows are used extensively by artists because they render quickly. Though not quite as precise as raytraced shadows, they're great for most general shadowing applications. To create depth map shadows, calculate one or more bitmaps showing the depths of the scene from the light's point of view. You then compare these bitmaps with the objects in the scene to determine which areas are in the shadow. These parameters are controlled using attributes to determine the size and placement of the map.

Determines the size of the depth map. Larger sizes produce sharper, more accurate shadows, but add to rendering time and memory usage.

The amount of filtering that is used on the shadow. Higher numbers produce shadows with softer edges.

An offset value used to move the shadow slightly away from the object. This is used to prevent shadows from overlapping the surface of the object. Default is 0.001, a very small number.

When rendering extremely large scenes, you may have to buffer depth maps to the hard disk.

Used primarily with point lights, this allows you to create multiple depth maps for lights that cover a wide area.

The color of the shadow

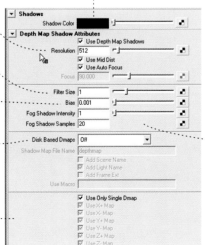

Fog parameters are used for creating volumetric shadows when fog is turned on.

Adjusting Depth Map Shadows

The two most important parameters to understand when working with depth map shadows are the resolution and the filter. Resolution determines the size of the map, which covers the width of the light cone. Filter controls the soft edge of the shadow. The larger the map, the more accurate the shadow. The larger the filter, the more softening. Softening, however, is relative to the resolution, so larger depth map resolutions require more filtering to get the same softness.

Although large maps are more accurate, they take up more memory when rendering. The size of the map depends on the cone angle of the light. If the light covers an area the size of the image, the depth map should be approximately the size of the image. Sometimes smaller maps are preferred, because they can produce softer shadows with less filtering.

Resolution = 256,
Filter size = 0

Resolution = 256,
Filter size = 2

Resolution = 256,
Filter size = 4

Resolution = 512,
Filter size = 2

Resolution = 512,
Filter size = 4

Resolution = 1024,
Filter size = 2

Depth Map Focus

The main issue that affects shadow map size is the cone angle of the spotlight. A wider spotlight spreads the same depth map over a wider area. Very wide spotlights may require large depth maps to avoid pixellation.

You can use Focus, which concentrates the map only in the area needed to cast the shadow, to get the most out of each and every depth map.

Auto Focus limits the size of the depth map to the size of the light's cone angle or to the outer edges of every object in the scene, whichever is smaller. Toggling Auto Focus off lets you manually control the angle of focus for the depth map.

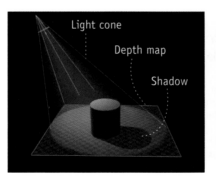

The depth map of a light usually covers the entire area cast by the light's cone. This may waste parts of the depth map, such as in this case, in which only one object needs a shadow.

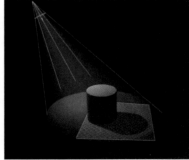

When Focus is used, the depth map can be adjusted to include only a portion of the scene, thus maximizing the depth map and creating better shadows.

TIP   If some shadows in a scene do not move, you might want to save rendering time by saving and reusing the depth maps. To do so, set the Disk Based Dmaps attribute from the drop-down list in the light's Attributes panel. When depth maps are saved to the disk, they are calculated once for the first frame and then used in each subsequent frame. This can save a lot of render time on large scenes. Depth maps are saved in the renderData/depth folder.

Raytraced Shadows

Raytraced shadows work by tracing the actual beams of light through the scene. This is more computationally expensive than simple depth map shadows, but raytraced shadows prove to be more accurate. They can create shadows for transparent objects, and they are also easier to set up, as you do not have to calculate map sizes. In order for raytraced shadows to render, you must turn on Raytracing in the Render Settings window.

Determines the diameter of the area emitting the shadow rays. A larger radius creates softer shadows. Area lights do not have this setting, because the radius is determined by the size of the area light.

Determines the number of transparent surfaces through which the shadow rays can pass

Determines the number of rays cast from this area. More rays create less-grainy and better-looking shadows, but increase rendering time.

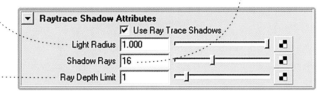

Raytraced shadows have three main attributes.

Creating raytraced shadows is simply a matter of deciding how sharp or soft the shadow needs to be. A small light radius combined with a small number of shadow rays creates sharp shadows; larger values soften the shadows.

Light Radius = 0
Shadow Rays = 1

Light Radius = 1.0
Shadow Rays = 1

Light Radius = 1.0
Shadow Rays = 32

Area Light, Shadow Rays = 16

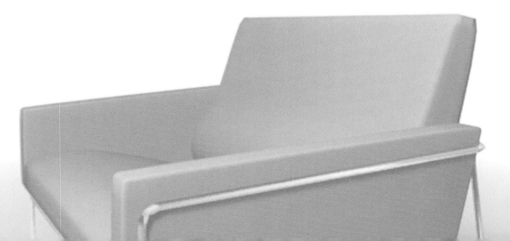

Shadow Linking

With raytraced shadows, you can control which lights cause specific objects to emit shadows. Controlling which objects cast raytraced shadows can dramatically improve render times. By default, all objects will cast shadows by any given light. If you link the light to a group of objects, then only those objects are included in raytraced shadow calculations.

To make a shadow link, select a light and then Shift+select objects. Choose Lighting/Shading → Make Shadow Links. To break a shadow link, select a light and the objects, and choose Lighting/Shading → Break Shadow Links.

Lighting Effects
Decay

By default, lights in Maya illuminate all objects equally, no matter how far they are from the light. In the real world, however, the intensity of a light decays with distance. To create more natural lighting that falls off over distance, you can select Decay Rate in the light's Attributes panel. There are three types of decay:

Linear falls off directly with distance.

Quadratic falls off as the square of the distance. This is the same as real-world lighting.

Cubic falls off with the cube of the distance, allowing for decay that's faster than real life.

When decay is added to a light, you almost always need to increase the intensity of the light to illuminate the scene. When using quadratic or cubic decay, you may have to increase the light intensity by several orders of magnitude to illuminate the scene.

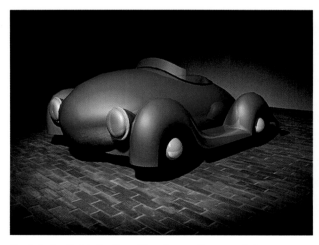

By default, lights in Maya illuminate all areas of the scene equally. The spotlight in this scene illuminates the back wall as much as the front fender of the car, even though the wall is farther away.

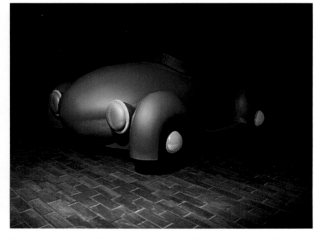

Decay causes the light intensity to fade according to distance; the scene is darker closer to the light source.

Intensity Curves

Another way to control the way light changes over distance is to use intensity curves. These are much more controllable than just simple decay and allow you to draw curves that can increase or decrease light intensity according to distance. The Intensity Curve tool is terrific for putting light into specific places in a scene.

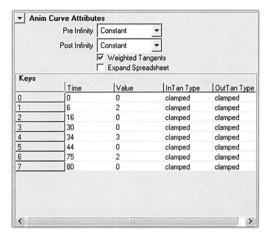

The intensity curve can be controlled using the spreadsheet in the Attributes panel. This allows you to enter distances and light intensities.

Another way to control the curve is to choose Window → Animation Editors → Graph Editor and edit the curve.

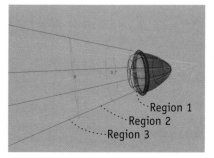

The result is a light that can vary according to distance. Although this is an extreme example, you can certainly simplify the curve to create specific light decays or highlights.

Decay Regions

Decay Regions is a way to turn a light on and off according to distance. Unlike Intensity Curves, you can adjust the values interactively using the Show Manipulator tool.

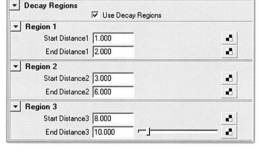

Decay Regions, in the light's Attributes panel, has the ability to turn the light on and off at three places.

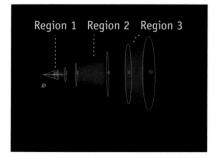

Decay regions do not have curves; they are simply on and off points.

Decay regions are good for lights that need to start away from the initial source of a light. This car headlight has a light source behind the face or surface of the headlight. Decay regions ensure the light starts at the front of the headlight.

The final result has the light coming from the front of the headlights rather than from behind them.

Projectors

Lights can also be used to project images on parts of the scene, much like a slide projector. This is accomplished by using a map in the color channel. This can be anything from a bitmap to a procedural texture, such as a ramp.

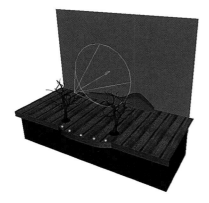

The spotlight in this scene is set to be used as a projector to cast an image. The bitmap of the night sky is placed in the spotlight's color channel, and the result casts the sky on the backdrop.

Fog

One way to make lights more visible is to use fog. Fog simulates the effect of light through a dusty or smoky room and can be used for dramatic effects. Fog can be used on spotlights, volume lights, or point lights. Fog in a spotlight takes up a cone shape, but point light fog can have a specific radius and falloff, for creating fog in a specific volume.

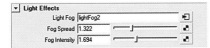

The fog settings in the Light Effects panel control two parameters. Fog Spread determines how the fog brightness varies across the light. A low number puts the densest part of the fog in the center of the cone; a high number pushes it toward the edges. Fog Intensity controls the brightness of the fog's color. Point lights have an additional slider for the radius of the fog.

Creating fog also creates a fog node. This controls the color of the fog as well as the fog density, or how thick the fog appears.

When combined with shadows, fog can create some dramatic effects.

Optical FX

Many times you need to make a light source visible. To do so, you use Maya's Optical FX, which allows you to add effects such as glow, halos, and lens flares to a light. Clicking to the right of the Light Glow attribute in the light's Attributes panel creates an Optical FX node.

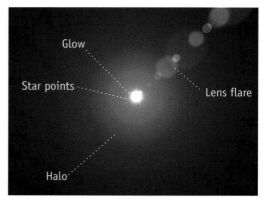

A thumbnail version of the final effect. This helps you to visualize the effect without having to render tests.

The basic parameters of the effect. There are toggles for Glow Type and Lens Flare, as well as drop-down menus to determine the type of glow and halo. This is the place to specify the number of star points (if any) and their relative brightness.

These attributes control the character of the glow effect. Color and intensity can be adjusted here. Glow Spread determines the size of the glow. Glow Noise and Glow Radial Noise can give the effect a less regular look.

Controls the color and size of the halo.

Controls the color of the lens flare, its intensity, as well as its size.

Optical FX components include glow, star points, halos, and lens flares. You can mix and match these to create all sorts of effects.

Area lights create rectangular glows that are the size of the light, making them useful for simulating such things as fluorescent fixtures or light panels.

Light Linking

Light linking gives you precise control over lighting on an object-by-object basis. This lets you assign lights to specific objects or parts of the scene, allowing for the optimum lighting for each object. Choose Lighting/Shading → Light Linking Editor to display two options. Light-Centric allows you to choose a light and then select which objects it illuminates. Object-Centric allows you to choose an object and specify which lights affect that object.

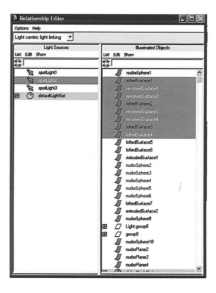

Lighting a Scene

1 Open the file Ch05Stage-Start.mb on the CD.

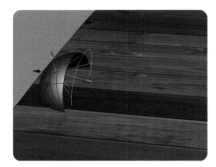

2 Start with the footlights. Create a spotlight and place it inside the sconces on the floor. Angle the light down slightly and turn up the intensity.

3 Render a test of this one light. It should illuminate just the floor.

4 Duplicate this light and populate the other sconces with lights.

5 Render a test. The additional lights add too much light and completely blow out the scene.

6 Since we liked the basic light, all we need to do to fix the problem is to limit the light to just the floor area, but not the objects in the background. Turn on Decay for all the lights. Set the lights to Linear Decay, and render a test.

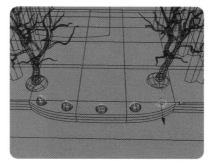

7 Let's light one of the trees. First, create a spotlight to cast a shadow. Keep it high and to the right of the tree, so the shadow falls on the stage. Use Look Through Selected to adjust the position of the light.

8 Render a test and tweak the shadow until it looks right. In this case, we used raytraced shadows because the castle has transparency in the texture map. A depth map shadow does not work with transparency.

9 Create a light to illuminate the tree itself. Since this scene is supposed to be moody, some under-lighting will do the trick. Create a yellow spotlight, and aim it up toward the tree.

10 A test render shows good light on the tree, but the light spills out onto the curtains and the rest of the scene.

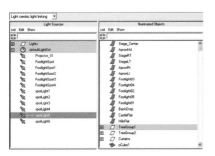

11 This can be fixed using light linking. Choose Lighting/Shading → Light Linking Editor → Light-Centric. Select the spot-light, and turn it on only for the tree model (TreeGroup1).

12 The result is a well-lit tree with a nice shadow. Repeat this process for the tree on the other side of the stage. The result should be two well-lit trees.

13 Add a spotlight for the castle. Since this is a night scene, the light is given a blue color. Adjust the light so that it hits the castle. Turn off shadows, since we should not need them for this object.

14 Render some tests and adjust the light so that the castle pops from the background.

15 Create the projector for the backdrop. Create a spotlight and give it a fairly wide cone angle, enough so the light covers the entire backdrop.

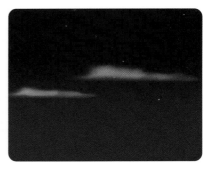

16 Add the Sky.tga image map to the color channel of the light. Render a test to make sure the bitmap is oriented in the proper direction. If not, adjust the UV mapping of the bitmap.

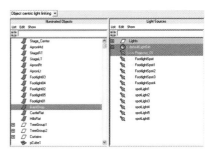

17 The light illuminates every-thing, and all we really want is to illuminate the backdrop. Again, we can use light linking to solve this problem. Choose Lighting/Shading → Light Linking Editor → Object-Centric. Select the backdrop object and assign the projector light to it, leaving all other lights off.

18 Render some tests and tweak the lighting until you're happy with it. The final file is called Ch05StageFinal.mb on the CD; this file has a basic stage scene.

6

Rendering

Rendering is the process whereby your Maya scenes come together into an image. Much like printing film in the darkroom, you truly create an image by rendering it. Creating good renders involves knowing a little bit about the technology behind the scenes, such as the way lights and cameras interact, as well as the way Maya and mental ray smooth and anti-alias images. mental ray provides advanced lighting simulations to create global illumination and caustics. Although knowing the technology can get you to the point where you can render almost anything, it's your artist's eye that puts this knowledge to use and makes the difference between a good image and a truly great one.

Cameras

Cameras in Maya are similar to real-world cameras. In addition to controlling what you see through viewports, they allow you to take virtual photographs, or renders, of a scene. Cameras in Maya have controls such as focal length and aperture as well as f-stop and shutter speed for creating effects such as depth of field and motion blur. Maya cameras, however, don't use film, so shutter speed and f-stop do nothing to affect the exposure of the image.

Types of Cameras

Although all cameras in Maya share the same sets of attributes, you'll see three types of cameras listed when you choose Create → Cameras. The only difference between these cameras and the other Maya cameras is the way they can be manipulated in the scene. You can also set these differences in the camera's Attribute Editor.

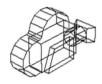

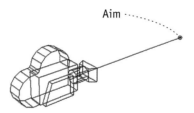

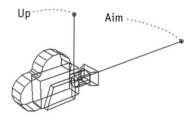

Camera is a basic camera that can be controlled using translation and rotation.

Camera and Aim create a camera, along with an aim point. The camera always points to this point in space. This makes positioning the camera simply a matter of translating the camera and the aim point, rather than rotating the camera. This can be useful when the camera is following the moving object. If the aim point follows the object, the camera will too.

Camera, Aim, and Up add a third point that is used when you need to animate side-to-side rotation of the camera, such as when banking around a curve.

Focal Length

The focal length of a lens determines the distance it takes for the lens to focus the image to a point. The focal length also determines how much of the scene can be focused, which is called the angle of view. In Maya, these two parameters are directly linked: as the Focal Length option increases, the Angle Of View option decreases.

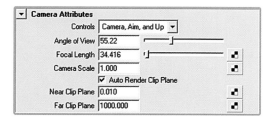

Focal Length and Angle Of View are set using the Camera Attributes panel. This is also where you set clipping planes.

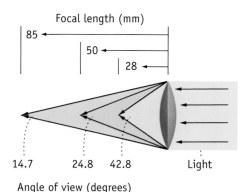

The closer the focal point is to the lens, the wider the angle of view.

Shorter focal lengths mean that objects must be closer to the camera to fill the field of view. Extremely short focal lengths can distort the perspective of a scene, and long ones tend to flatten it.

Focal Length 15mm, Angle Of View 100.3. An extremely short focal length creates a fish-eye effect.

Focal Length 28mm, Angle Of View 42.8. A standard wide-angle lens reduces this effect.

Focal Length 50mm, Angle Of View 24.7. A 50mm lens is one of the most common and is good for most general applications.

Focal Length 135mm, Angle Of View 9.3. Longer lenses can be good for portraits, but at very long lengths, the lens might flatten the scene too much.

TIP If the focal length of a real-world camera goes to infinity, the camera sees everything with no perspective. Such a camera is called an *orthographic* camera and is used for the familiar top, front, and side viewports. In a camera's attributes under Orthographic Views is a setting to create an orthographic camera. This can be handy if you need to create a bottom or a right-side viewport.

Clipping Planes

Clipping planes define the distances over which the camera will work. Typically, Maya sets this automatically by toggling Auto Render Clip Plane on. The clipping plane then includes the closest and farthest objects in the scene. Clipping planes can, however, be used for a number of tasks, such as dividing a scene into layers for rendering.

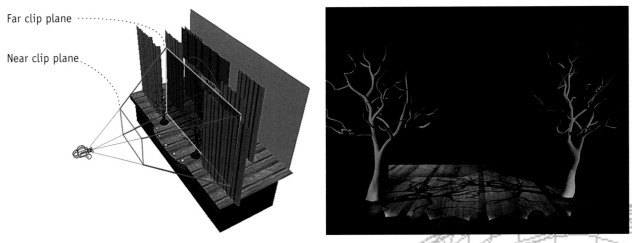

Clipping planes determine what the camera sees. In this case, the clipping plane is set to see only the front part of the stage, as shown by the rendered view.

You might also want to adjust a clipping plane manually when you are modeling. For example, you might need to work on part of a model in wireframe without being distracted by all the vertices on the back side of the model. By setting the clipping plane close to the working plane, you can hide the far side of the model.

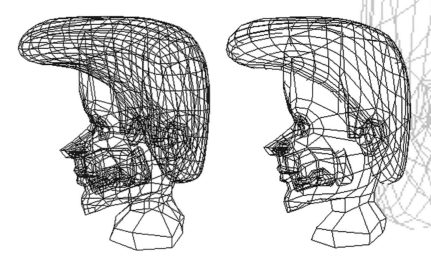

(left) When working in wireframe, wires on the far side of the model can sometimes be distracting. (right) Setting the clipping plane to view the part of the model closest to the camera can make things easier to see.

Depth of Field

Depth of field simulates how a real-world camera focuses. Focus is important in cameras because it allows the photographer to guide the viewer's eye to the important parts of the scene. Cameras tend to focus objects in a range of distances. A low depth of field means the range is narrow; fewer parts of the scene will be in focus. Conversely, the higher the depth of field, the more of the scene will be in focus.

In a real camera, the f-stop determines the depth of field. The f-stop number is determined by the size of the lens and the size of the aperture, which is the opening that allows light to reach the film. Higher f-stop numbers mean smaller apertures, which give a greater depth of field.

F-stop is the primary parameter used to determine the depth of field. Lower f-stop numbers mean that more of the image will be out of focus; higher numbers put more of the image into focus.

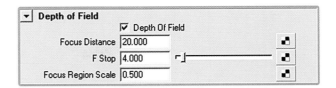

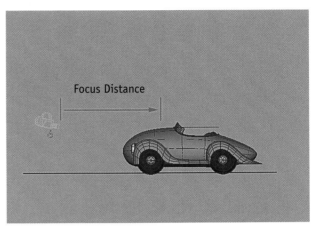

Focus distance is the distance to the focal point, usually a point of interest in the scene. Depth of field blurs the image behind and in front of this point. The amount of blurring depends on the values of F Stop and Focus Region Scale.

F Stop = 1

F Stop = 2

F Stop = 4

F Stop = 16

In addition to F Stop, Maya also has a parameter called Focus Region Scale. This is primarily used to fine-tune focus effects. The number is essentially a multiplier. Numbers less than one reduce the depth of field, and numbers more than one expand it, causing less blurring.

Focus Region Scale = 0.5

Focus Region Scale = 1.0

Focus Region Scale = 2.0

Motion Blur

Another camera effect is motion blur. In the real world, it takes time to expose a frame of film. If the subject moves during this exposure time, the resulting image is blurred. In Maya, there is no such thing as film speed, so motion blur has to be simulated. This is done in two places. First, by using the Shutter Speed attribute in the camera's Attributes panel. Second, by configuring the Motion Blur attributes in the Render Settings window. Maya has two types of motion blur.

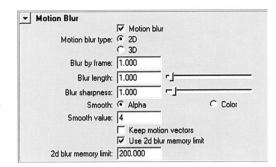

Motion blur is set in the Render Settings window. 3D Motion Blur is set to on or off, but 2D Motion Blur has a number of options. Blur By Frame controls the amount of blur in numbers of frames. Blur Length controls the intensity of the blur, and Blur Sharpness controls the spread of the blur.

Unblurred shadow

Depth map shadow:
Size = 256, Filtering = 5

2D Motion Blur is a postrender process that simply blurs the pixels of the scene. It renders quickly, but the results are not completely accurate. It is best used for objects in the background of the image.

3D Motion Blur takes into account the movement of the geometry itself as well as the shutter angle of the camera. It renders slower than 2D Motion Blur, but is more physically accurate and suitable for foreground work. A limitation of Maya motion blur is that it does not blur shadows. It also does not blur raytracing or particles.

If an image includes shadows, it's best to use a depth map shadow with a high degree of filtering. This gives a soft shadow that appears to be blurred.

Motion Blur in mental ray

Motion blur in mental ray is more robust than Maya's motion blur, and it has no limitations. mental ray blurs anything in the scene: shaders, textures, lights, shadows, reflections, refractions, and caustics. There are two types of motion blur in mental ray:

Linear mode calculates motion blur for every object in the scene, but does not consider shape changes. This is fine for most applications.

Exact mode adds extra calculations to consider changes in the shape of an object. This is a little bit slower, but good for fast-moving characters or creatures that tend to change shape quickly.

Motion blur for mental ray is more accurate than Maya's motion blur and can blur such things as shadows and reflections.

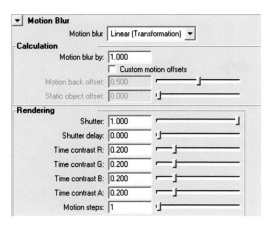

Like Maya's 3D Motion Blur, mental ray uses the camera's shutter angle to determine the amount of blur. This is modified by the Motion Blur attributes in the Render Settings window. Custom Motion Offsets enables the Motion Back Offset and Static Object Offset fields, which define time steps for capturing the motion blur data. Motion Blur By is a multiplier to amplify the effect. Shutter and Shutter Delay define exactly how the shutter closes to simulate real-world cameras. Time Contrast determines how much the motion blur is sampled per image channel; lower numbers increase quality and rendering time.

Render Settings

Much of the rendering process in Maya is controlled in the Render Settings window (choose Window → Rendering Editors → Render Settings). This window has two tabs. The first is a common panel that you can use to specify the size and format of the render and the filenames. The second tab is unique to each renderer: Maya Software, Maya Hardware, mental ray, and Maya Vector.

The renderer is selected here: Maya Software, Maya Hardware, mental ray, or Maya Vector.

A tab holds custom settings for each renderer.

The name and type of the rendered files are selected here.

The start and end frames to be rendered, as well as how many frames to skip and number of frames to pad.

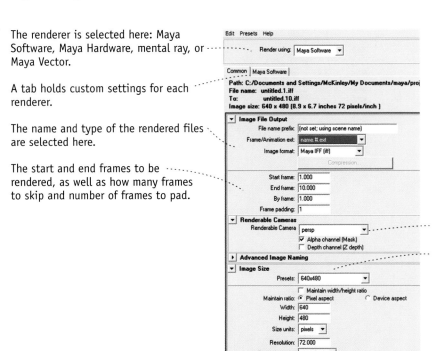

The camera to be used when rendering.

The size of the rendered image. You can select from a number of presets for most film and video types, as well as create your own.

Render View

The Render View window (choose Window → Rendering Editors → Render View) is where Maya shows you what it has rendered. It opens automatically whenever a rendering operation is launched, either from the menus or the Status line.

A menu to save and load image files.

Changes the way the final image is viewed.

Allows you to render the entire image, a region, or a different camera or viewport.

Options for rendering images using Maya's Interactive Photorealistic Rendering (IPR).

Options to open the Render Settings window as well as change the renderer.

Options to turn RGB channels on/off as well as luminance and dithering.

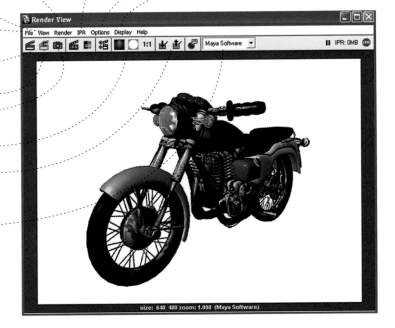

Render Image Renders the entire image.

Render Region Renders only the selected region.

IPR Renders using IPR.

Channels Displays the RGB or alpha channels.

Buffers Allows you to create a buffer of images. Moving the slider on the bottom of the window steps through the buffer.

Renderer Chooses the renderer to use.

Render Region

Rendering regions is a great way to speed up the time it takes to do test renders. It allows you to select a region of the image and render only the pixels within that region. This can be handy when tweaking lighting or texturing.

Render region

Regions are selected by clicking and dragging the mouse over the image in render view. Choosing Render Region from the menu or toolbar renders only the selected pixels.

Interactive Photorealistic Rendering

IPR is similar to Render Region, except IPR is completely interactive. It stores all the information relating to each pixel of the image and then uses that to update the image quickly as parameters are changed. IPR works with both the Maya software renderer and mental ray.

There are a few limitations to IPR. When using the Maya software renderer, it does not render raytracing, particles, or motion blur. mental ray does, however, support particles and raytracing in IPR. For unsupported features, you can use the standard render options, including Render Region. You can launch IPR from render view, with the IPR icon on the toolbar, or by choosing IPR → IPR Render → Current.

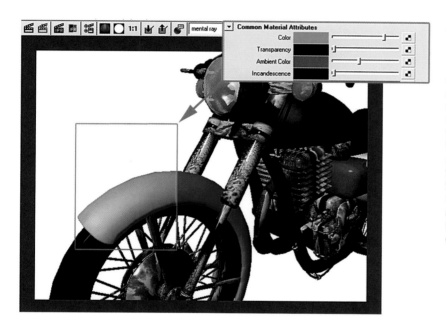

IPR works similarly to Render Region. In the Render View window, click and drag to define a region. That area renders. As surface parameters in the scene are changed, such as the color of this fender, the IPR region updates automatically to reflect the changes.

When IPR is used with the Maya software renderer, raytracing is not supported, but you can choose (in the shortcut menu) whether IPR will update shading and lighting as well as glows. mental ray's shortcut menu offers the option of calculating raytracing as part of the IPR solution.

> **TIP**   Maya offers a basic batch rendering utility that is accessible by choosing Render →
> Batch Render. Whatever options are selected in the Render Settings window are rendered, with
> the results showing up in the current project's folder. Batch Render has one option for the num-
> ber of rendering threads. This can be handy on a multiple-processor machine to reduce the ren-
> dering overhead so that you can continue to work as the scene renders.

Maya Software Renderer

Maya's software renderer is the default renderer for the software and is a good general-purpose renderer. It's the renderer used in most of this book, so you've already had some experience with it. Maya's software renderer is also the most tightly integrated renderer available to Maya, and any feature in the renderer can be connected seamlessly with any other feature in Maya. The renderer supports both scanline and raytracing, so only those parts of the scene that need the extra processing power of raytracing receive it.

When Maya Software is the chosen renderer, all its options are controlled through the Maya Software panel in the Render Settings window.

Anti-Aliasing

Anti-aliasing controls how the renderer smooths and blends jagged-edge pixels. Getting good-looking edges is important to achieving superior-quality render-ings, so Maya provides a wide degree of control over the way images can be anti-aliased.

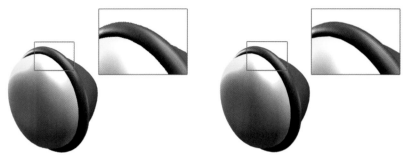

Low anti-aliasing (left) vs. high anti-aliasing (right). Notice the jagged edges on the left; everything is smooth on the right.

Maya provides a number of presets. Selecting one of these may be all you need to get the right results. You can also choose Custom and set the attributes manually.

Preset quality controls affect the way edges are anti-aliased.

Controls the amount of oversampling of the image. Maya uses an adaptive method for shading pixels, so the settings for shading and for 3D motion blur have a range. The more contrast in the image, the higher the sampling rate. The ranges limit the minimum and maximum amount of oversampling.

Determines exactly how the adaptive sampling methods work. Lower numbers increase the sampling, and each channel of the image can have its own controls. This is particularly useful for tweaking the contrast of alpha channel mattes.

Blurs or softens the entire rendered image to help eliminate jagged edges as well as improve the edges of thin lines and highlights. The filtering method is selected using a drop-down menu. Multipixel filtering renders much faster than increasing the number of samples, so it is often advantageous to increase the values here first.

Raytracing

In addition to shadows, raytracing in Maya's software renderer allows it to create highly realistic reflections and refractions. Raytracing works by tracing rays of light from the camera throughout the scene. Raytracing is configured in two places. First, the shader must have a reflective or transparent material. Second, the renderer must have raytracing enabled.

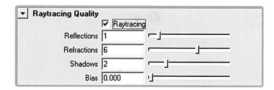

Raytracing is configured by setting the number of times a raytracing ray can reflect or refract off a surface. This can be set both in the material and in the Render Settings window.

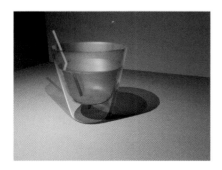 

(left) When the number of reflections is set to 1, one object can reflect another, but not much else. (right) Adding more reflections allows objects to reflect one another's reflections, adding to the sense of realism.

 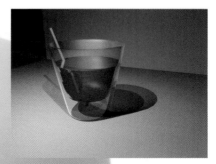

The number of refractions needed in a scene can add up quickly. (left) We have at least six surfaces to refract: two sides of the front of the glass, the front and back of the liquid, and two more sides on the back of the glass. (center) When the number of refractions is set to 2, only the front part of the glass refracts. (right) Setting it to 4 refracts the front of the glass and the liquid, but not the far side of the glass.

mental ray Renderer

mental ray for Maya is an excellent renderer that has become a standard at many studios around the world. mental ray is much more robust than Maya's software renderer when it comes to creating highly realistic effects. Global Illumination allows mental ray to simulate the way light bounces off diffuse surfaces. This can create a much-softer and more-realistic scene. Caustics simulate the way light reflects or passes through complex objects and can simulate such materials as glass, water, and reflective metals.

Maya has fairly tight integration with mental ray, meaning much of it is invisible to the average user. Shaders, lights, and cameras from Maya transfer over to mental ray with little effort. For additional control, cameras, lights, objects, and shaders all have mental ray attributes that become active when mental ray is used as the renderer. Additional mental ray rendering features, such as Global Illumination and caustics, can be used on most Maya scenes as well.

Basic controls over the mental ray renderer are located in the Render Settings window under the mental ray tab. Many of the basic parameters are similar to Maya's software renderer. These attributes include settings for anti-aliasing, shadows, and raytracing.

Like Maya's software renderer, mental ray has a number of useful presets that are helpful when creating previews or getting ready for the final render.

Sets the minimum and maximum number of samples per pixel to use when calculating anti-aliasing.

Blurs or softens the entire rendered image to help eliminate jagged edges as well as improve the edges of thin lines and highlights. The filtering method is selected using a drop-down menu. Options include Box, Triangle, Gauss, Mitchell, and Lanczos. Gauss is the most accurate but renders the slowest.

Determines exactly how the adaptive sampling methods work. Lower numbers increase the sampling, and each channel of the image can have its own controls. This is particularly useful for tweaking the contrast of alpha channel mattes.

Sample Lock locks the positions at which mental ray samples the pixels. Usually the best way to sample. Jitter introduces a random effect and can reduce or eliminate some rendering artifacts, such as moiré patterns.

Sets the attributes for raytracing. Allows for the maximum number of reflections and refractions, as well as the total depth for both combined. You can also specify how deep the renderer traces shadows, whether to use scanline rendering for increased speed, and which faces of the objects to render—back, front, or both.

Controls for mental ray shadows. mental ray uses three methods. Simple is the fastest and is good for most applications, Sort is used only when using custom shadow shaders, and Segments is used for volume effects, such as fur, particles, and smoke.

Global Illumination

Global Illumination is a rendering method used to create highly realistic lighting and shading. It simulates the actual scattering of photons of light around the scene. Although it is computationally expensive, the results are often worth the extra processor time.

Global Illumination is controlled in two places. First, the light must be set up to cast photons; then the renderer must be configured to accept these photons and render the results.

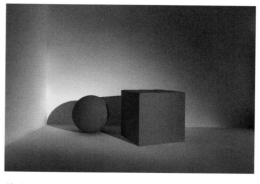

Global Illumination on a scene

The color of the photons. It is usually best to match this color to the light color, but it can be varied for other types of effects.

Allows the light to emit photons so that it can become a light source for global illumination.

The amount of energy emitted by the light source. Higher energies create stronger global illumination (or caustics) lighting. This value also depends on the size of the scene. Larger scenes require more energy to get the same lighting effect as a smaller scene.

The mental ray attributes for a spotlight

Similar to decay, it allows you to set how quickly the photons lose energy. The default value of 2.0 sets the energy to decay at the inverse square of the distance, simulating reality. Higher values limit the energy, and lower values effectively intensify it. Values below 1.0 can create noisy results.

The actual number of photons emitted when calculating global illumination. More photons create more-accurate results, but at the cost of more rendering time.

The actual number of photons emitted when calculating caustics. More photons create more-accurate results, but at the cost of more rendering time.

Toggles the effect on or off.

The accuracy of the solution. Higher numbers create more physically accurate renders at the cost of rendering time. Values over 90 significantly increase render time.

Determines the maximum radius of global illumination photons, and values between 1 and 2 can eliminate graininess at the expense of blurring. When set to the default of 0, the optimum number is calculated automatically.

Used to control the intensity of caustics and global illumination through objects such as lenses.

Controls the maximum distance that mental ray projects photons. This allows Maya to stop calculating photons that fly off into empty space.

The maximum number of times a photon will bounce in a reflection or refraction. This needs to be adjusted to account for transparent or reflective surfaces.

Controls the maximum number of reflections and refractions that a photon will calculate.

The Global Illumination panel in the mental ray Render Settings window

Photons

There are two main lighting parameters to consider when setting up global illumination; photon intensity and number of photons. Intensity is the brightness of the light. The number of photons is similar to a sampling rate and affects the quality of the image. More photons produce more-accurate results, but at the cost of additional render time. For physically accurate renders, the number of photons can get incredibly high, into the millions.

(left) Photons = 500. When the number of photons is low, the individual spots of light can be seen. (center) Photons = 2000. As the number of photons increases, they start to blend. (right) Photons = 10,000. Eventually, the photons overlap, and the illumination can be seen. When using just photons to illuminate the scene, it can take millions of photons to completely smooth out the graininess.

Final Gathering

Final Gathering is used as a finishing tool for Global Illumination and can help reduce the need for high numbers of photons. In its simplest sense, it can be used as a blending algorithm, and it smooths and interpolates the light created by the photons to simulate a radiosity solution.

Final Gathering is similar to raytracing, but whereas raytracing traces light rays from the camera's point of view, Global Illumination starts at the light source and traces from there. Final Gathering rays are emitted from a light; when they hit a surface, mental ray calculates the way the rays are scattered, along with their new energies. This process is continued, and the secondary rays of light continue to bounce off other surfaces and so on, creating a soft and realistic lighting of the scene.

(left) Global Illumination photons are plainly visible in this scene; many more photons could be added, but at the cost of rendering time. (right) Final Gathering smooths out the graininess in this scene, creating a good final result.

Controls the size of the sample region for computing Final Gathering. When set to 0, the amounts are calculated automatically. For manual control, enter a value that is 10% of a scene's overall dimension for Max Radius; enter 10% of that for Min Radius, and then tweak from there.

Used to eliminate speckles and hot spots in the Final Gathering process. Higher numbers eliminate speckles, but at the cost of accuracy.

Numbers to control the start and stop of Final Gathering rays (but not Global Illumination photons). Used to limit the reach of indirect light.

Controls the number of times a Final Gathering ray bounces before stopping. Additional values control reflections and refractions.

Toggles the effect on or off.

Approximates the irradiance at each point in the scene as the photons are traced. This can help speed render times.

Controls quality of the final render by controlling the number of rays shown from each light at each Final Gathering step. Low numbers around 100 are good for previews; numbers above 1000 are good for final rendering. Large numbers can raise render times exponentially.

Final Gather	
☑ Final gather	
☐ Precompute photon lookup	
Final gather rays:	100
Min radius:	0.000
Max radius:	0.000
☐ View (Radii in pixel size)	
Final gather scale:	
Filter:	1
Falloff start:	0.000
Falloff stop:	0.000
Trace depth:	2
Trace reflection:	1
Trace refraction:	1
☐ Secondary diffuse bounces	
Rebuild final gather:	On
Final gather file:	
☐ Enable map visualizer	
☑ Preview final gather tiles	

The Final Gather panel in the mental ray Render Settings window

Photon Intensity

The second major attribute used to calculate global illumination is the photon intensity. This is roughly equivalent to a light's brightness. Photons, however, perform only indirect lighting, so increasing photon intensity will increase only the amount of indirect light in the scene. Photon intensity is also sensitive to the scale of the scene. Larger scenes need much larger intensities to get the same amount of lighting as a smaller scene.

Photon Intensity = 2000. At low intensities, photons don't do much to provide additional illumination.

Photon Intensity = 16,000. Increasing the photon intensity adds diffuse global illumination to the scene.

Photon Intensity = 75,000. At very high intensities, the diffuse light from the photons starts to overwhelm the direct lights in the scene.

With the direct light's intensity turned down to 0, the indirect light created strictly by the scene's photons can be seen.

Caustics

Caustics simulate the way light refracts through a complex surface or reflects off it. Caustics are useful in simulating such surfaces as water, glass, and metals. Working with caustics can be a little bit tricky because a number of variables affect the way the final render looks. The photon intensity and the exponent of the falloff, as well as the distance of the light, number of photons, and the materials of the objects all affect the outcome.

A number that determines the physical accuracy of the caustics solution. Higher numbers produce more-accurate renders at the cost of render time. Default is 64.

Toggles rendering of caustics on or off.

The radius of the volume used to render caustics. Generally this is the size of the scene, but it can be reduced to limit caustics to specific areas. At the default of 0, the value is calculated automatically.

Box is faster and generally makes caustics look sharper; Cone produces smoother results.

A number used by Caustic Filter when smoothing the caustics. Bigger numbers produce softer caustics.

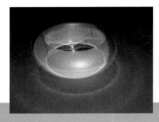

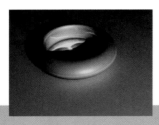

Refractive caustics simulate the transmission of light through a transparent material.

Reflective caustics simulate the reflection of light off a surface.

The Caustics And Global Illumination panel in the mental ray Render Settings window

Photon Intensity is probably the most important value when generating caustics. The intensity of caustics pretty much follows the intensity of the photons. When the value is too low, the caustics appear faint, but high numbers can easily blow out a render.

Photon Intensity = 4000, Exponent = 2.

Photon Intensity = 8000, Exponent = 2.

Photon Intensity = 16,000, Exponent = 2.

The position of the light is another important value to consider. By default, photon intensity decays at the square of the distance from the light. This means that placing the light twice as far away reduces the intensity of the photons by a factor of four. Conversely, moving the light twice as close quadruples the intensity.

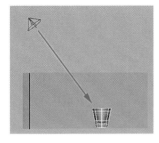

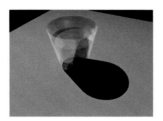

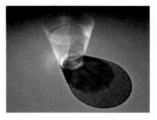

The distance of the light from the subject has a real effect on the strength of the caustic.

When the light is far away, the photons do not have enough energy to create a caustic. Increasing photon intensity could solve this problem.

As the light gets closer, the caustic becomes stronger.

When the light gets too close, the photon intensity is too much and starts to overexpose the image.

Finally, the Exponent attribute also plays a factor in how the caustic is generated. This number represents the exponential value at which the light energy decays. Generally, this is kept at the default of 2, which simulates the inverse square law and real-world lighting, but lower numbers can extend the power of the light, and higher numbers will limit it.

Exponent = 2.0. The light obeys the inverse square law, which simulates reality and is similar to the quadratic falloff on Maya lights.

Exponent = 1.0. The decay is linear, effectively making the photons more intense over a longer distance. In this case, the extra intensity blows out the image, but reducing photon energy can correct this. Lower exponents are good when you need to light a larger area or animate lights.

Exponent = 2.75. When the value approaches 3, the photons lose intensity at the cube of the distance, which produces a steep falloff that severely limits the light energy.

TIP For truly realistic lighting, it is a good idea to set the decay of the light to match that of the photons. If your photon exponent is 2, set your light to quadratic, for example.

Maya Vector Renderer

Maya's vector renderer uses mathematical formulae to represent color and shape in a rendered image rather than the typical raster graphics that other renderers output. Vector rendering is most useful when you need to export the color and shape vector data to an external program, such as Macromedia Flash or Adobe Illustrator. In addition, Maya can create animated vector files, such as the Flash .swf format, so that you can view 3D animations within a website.

Because a vector image is calculated rather than rasterized, you lose no quality when increasing the scale of the image. Maya gives you a wide variety of options that can drastically affect the performance and aesthetic of vector-rendered images.

Controls how straight or curved the outlines around rendered objects appear. The straighter the outlines, the greater the file size, and the more accurate the outlines appear relative to the polygons.

Determines how much detail will be rendered.

Various options to control how colors are represented when rendered.

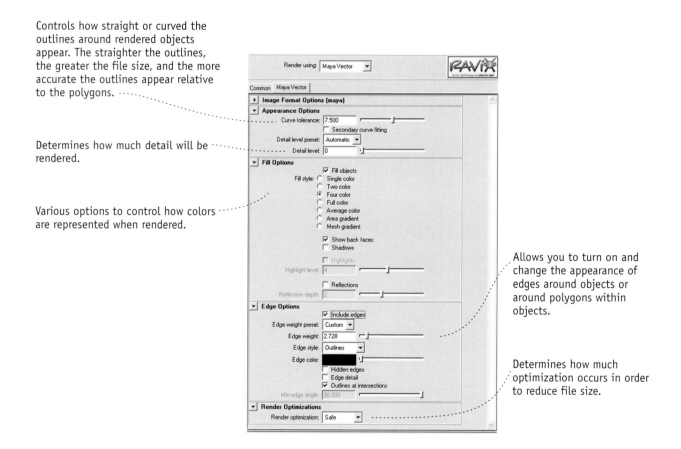

Allows you to turn on and change the appearance of edges around objects or around polygons within objects.

Determines how much optimization occurs in order to reduce file size.

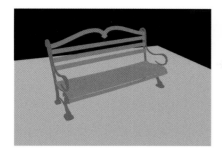

Single Color: Every mesh retains one averaged color.

Two Color: Every mesh retains two averaged colors and is influenced by the lighting.

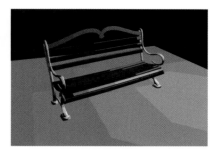

Four Color: Every mesh retains four averaged colors and is influenced by the lighting.

Full Color: Each polygon has one solid color and is influenced by the lighting.

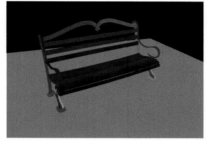

Average Color: Each surface has one averaged solid color and is influenced by the lighting.

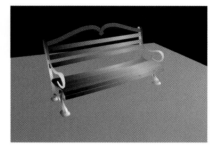

Area Gradient: Each surface has one radial gradient and is influenced by the lighting.

Mesh Gradient: Each polygon is filled with a linear gradient and is influenced by the lighting.

Selecting the Outlines Edge style draws an outline around the edges of objects.

Selecting the Entire Mesh Edge style draws an outline around every polygon within an object. Notice that although faces may be quadrangles in the model, all polygons are triangulated at render time. Therefore, any Entire Mesh style will always appear triangulated no matter how many n-sided polygons exist.

Hardware Rendering

Hardware rendering is the process of using your computer's graphics card to render images. There are two ways to use hardware rendering: the Maya hardware renderer and the hardware render buffer. Typically, hardware rendering is used for particle effects that cannot be rendered using the software renderer.

Maya Hardware Renderer

The Maya hardware renderer supports many of the standard texture maps (such as displacement, bump, blinn, ramp), lights, hardware particles, shadows, and other render nodes to deliver next-gen quality renders. Maya hardware rendering is generally faster than software rendering and is typically used over the hardware render buffer because of the hardware renderer's supported features. The Maya hardware renderer also supports batch rendering.

Serves as a good starting point for rendering the scene at a given quality.

Determines how many samples to use per pixel when anti-aliasing.

The method for calculating transparency on objects. Per Object yields faster results but may render incorrectly for complex objects. Per Polygon is more accurate but renders longer.

If the renderer cannot evaluate the shading network, the color and/or bump maps are baked into a new texture. Changing the resolution affects the quality of these textures.

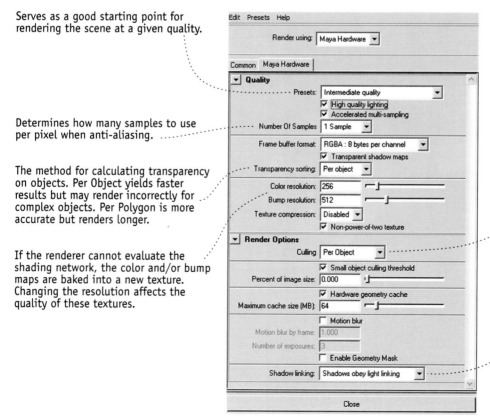

Controls how backface culling is handled when rendered. Per Object refers to culling attributes set for each object in the Render Stats. All Double Sided forces all objects to be rendered with double-sided polygons, while All Single Sided forces all objects to render single-sided polygons.

Determines whether shadows obey shadow linking, obey light linking, or ignore linking.

Hardware Render Buffer

The hardware render buffer is a rendering editor that allows you to quickly and easily preview hardware-rendered frames. Although it is good for previewing particle rendering, its lack of advanced hardware rendering features make the Maya hardware renderer the more common choice. To open the hardware render buffer, choose Window → Rendering Editors → Hardware Render Buffer.

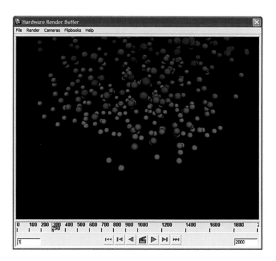

Toon Shading

Maya offers a set of tools that allows you to simulate a hand-drawn, cartoony shading style. Toon shading provides various fill styles, can create paint effects outlines, and contains various types of modifiers to fine-tune the cartoon look.

You can apply a toon fill shader through the Toon → Assign Fill Shader menu. These shaders are actually presets of similar toon shaders. Toon fill shading types include the following:

Solid Color: Each object with this shader assigned will display only one solid color.

Light Angle Two Tone: A ramp-based shader that bases its tonality on the light angle.

Shaded Brightness Two Tone: A ramp-based shader with two color values that bases its tonality on the diffuse shaded brightness.

Shaded Brightness Three Tone: A ramp-based shader with three color values that bases its tonality on the diffuse shaded brightness.

Dark Profile: A ramp-based shader that bases its tonality on the surface brightness. An incandescence ramp has a dark gray color, causing dark areas around the edges of the surface.

Circle Highlight: A ramp-based shader that bases its tonality on the surface brightness. A specular ramp controls a sharp white highlight that simulates shiny objects well.

Rim Light: A ramp-based shader that bases its tonality on the surface brightness. An incandescence ramp has a light color that creates a highlight on the edges of the surface.

Outlines

Outlines are a dynamic effect that creates borders around the edges of your scene objects. Because they are made from paint effects, their style, shape, and color can be easily modified in the Attribute Editor. To assign an outline, select an object and choose Toon → Assign Outline → Add New Outline. Alternatively, you can choose an existing outline paint effects object if one exists already.

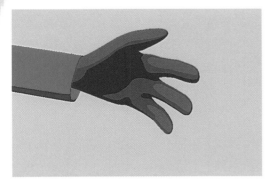

Toon render with no outlines

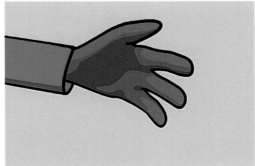

Toon render with outlines

Modifiers

A modifier is an object that can change the appearance of a toon outline. There are two volumes: sphere and cube. If a modifier's volume passes within an associated outline, the outline will change according to the modifier's attributes. To add a modifier, select a paint effects outline and choose Toon → Create Modifier.

An outline with no modifiers.

A modifier that increases the size of the outline is placed on the lamp pole.

Two modifiers are added to change the color of the outline. Notice how nicely the effect dissipates as the outline moves away from the modifier's origin.

Rendering Global Illumination

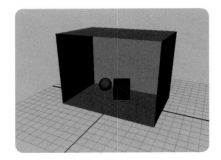

1 Open the file Ch06_GI_start.mb from the CD. This should contain a very simple scene with a cube and a sphere inside a box.

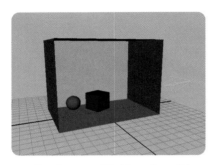

2 Create a spotlight and position it at the top right of the objects in the box.

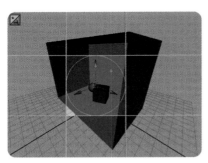

3 Select the light, and choose Panels → Look Through Selected in a viewport menu. Turn on the Manipulator tool and adjust the light so it shines directly on the objects.

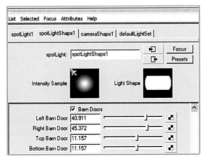

4 Use the Barn Doors light's Attributes panel to turn the light from a circular to a long rectangle shape.

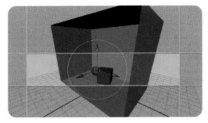

5 When viewed through the light, the result should look something like this. To see the effect of the barn doors, the Manipulator tool must be toggled on.

6 Select mental ray as the renderer and render a test. You should see a slit of light, but no global illumination.

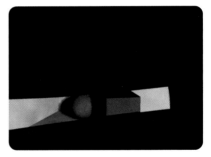

7 You configure Global Illumination in two places. First, you can turn

it on in the mental ray tab of the Render Settings window. You can also select the preset Preview Global-Illum.

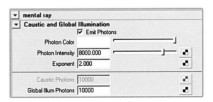

8 Select the light, and in the Attribute Editor turn on Emit Photons. Leave the values at the presets: Photon Intensity 8000, Exponent 2.0, and Number of Photons 10,000.

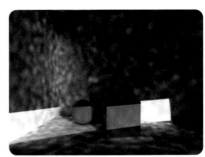

9 Render a test. This will show you the photons and look a little grainy, but it will give you a general idea of how the scene will be lit. In this case, it looks a little dark.

10 Set Photon Intensity to 24,000. This brings up the level of the diffuse light in the room. If you want to take down the graininess, you can bring up the number of photons. This was rendered with 20,000 photons.

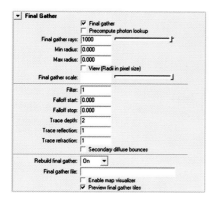

11 Now it's time to add Final Gathering to smooth out and blend the photons of the scene. In the Render Settings menu, turn on Final Gather and leave the values at the default.

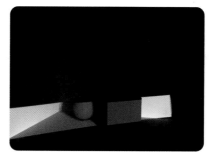

12 Render a test. This looks pretty good, but the shadows are grainy. This is because we're still using the default depth map shadows on the light. In the spotlight's Attributes panel, select Raytraced Shadows.

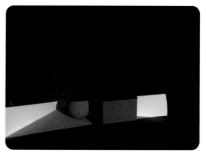

13 Render another test. This looks pretty good. Adjust the final anti-aliasing settings for a final render, and render the final scene.

Rendering Caustics

Caustics are the best way to realistically render such things as glass and water. Rendering caustics, however, can require a lot of fine-tuning. The process is similar to creating global illumination. Lights are set to emit photons, and then the intensities are adjusted until the scene looks good.

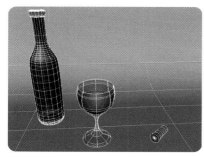

1 Open the file Ch06_Caustics_start.mb from the CD. This file contains a simple scene with a glass of wine and a bottle illuminated by a single spotlight.

2 Select the mental ray renderer from the Render Settings menu and render the scene. The depth map shadows don't work with the scene.

3 Select the spotlight, and turn on Raytraced Shadows in the Attributes panel.

4 Render another test. The shadows look good, but we need to allow for more refractions.

5 In the Render Settings window, turn up the number of refractions, reflections, and shadows. For the glass to render properly, the key number here is six refractions, but we can go higher just in case.

6 Another render has the scene looking fairly good. Now it's time to add the caustics. We need to turn it on both in the light and the renderer.

the scene to get the effect. Increase the light's Photon Intensity to 24,000.

10 Render another test. This is getting close, but we could use a little more contrast. We could continue to increase light energy, but let's play with Exponent instead. Turn the light's exponent to 1.5. This will let the light's photons lose energy at a slower rate.

11 Another render test shows we went a little bit too far. Let's split the difference, and back off the exponent to 1.7.

12 This is looking pretty good and is probably suitable for final rendering.

7 In the Render Settings window, turn on Caustics.

8 In the spotlight's Attributes panel, turn on Emit Photons. Leave the values at the default: Photon Intensity 8000, Exponent 2.0, and Number of Photons 10,000.

9 Render a test. The caustics really aren't showing up. We need to get more light energy into

13 Increase the anti-aliasing preset in the Render Settings window to Production. If you want, you can continue to tweak the image. Adding more photons can sharpen the caustics and eliminate some of the graininess. In this case, we went fairly high and rendered the scene with 250,000 photons. Rendering a final version may take a little while.

Paint Effects

P aint Effects is a 2D and 3D paint tool that can create anything from a simple brush stroke to complete 3D environments. The tool works like a paintbrush, but in addition to painting color, you can also paint geometry. The tool can work in 2D much like a traditional painting package, but its full power is realized in 3D. You can paint anything from grass and flowers to underwater scenes, lightning bolts, fire, cityscapes, and anything else you can imagine. The tool has a robust library of brushes that can be used to create many effects, and its versatility reaches a new level when these presets are customized to create new and novel brushes.

Paint Effects Basics

Much like Artisan, Paint Effects uses a brush-driven interface. A Paint Effects brush can paint anything from a solid color to actual geometry.

Paint Effects works with two main components, strokes and brushes. Painting in a viewport creates strokes; these are essentially curves, either on a surface or in space. Connected to these strokes are brushes; these are what the renderer sees and can be anything from a paint stroke to complex geometry.

By separating the stroke from the actual image, you have a tremendous degree of flexibility, allowing brushes to be edited and changed after the fact. Grass that was painted as short and green can quickly be changed to long and brown.

To use Paint Effects on an object, select the object, and choose Paint Effects → Make Paintable.

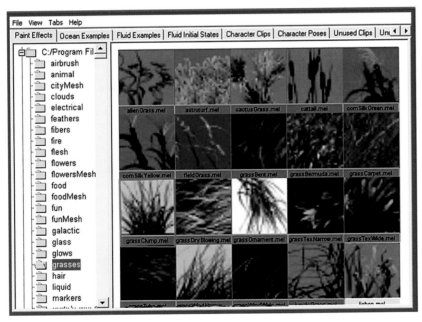

Open Visor (choose Window → General Editors → Visor) and select a Paint Effects brush.

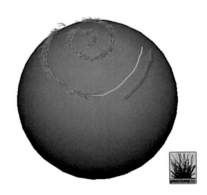

Paint a stroke on the object. As the stroke is painted, the brush applies the desired effect (in this case, grass).

Rendering the scene shows realistic grass.

Brushes

A Paint Effects brush is incredibly flexible because a brush can have hundreds of attributes, allowing it to achieve a wide array of effects. When a brush is attached to a stroke via the painting interface, its attributes are used to calculate the look and behavior of the brush. In its basic sense, a Paint Effects brush is simply a preset that stores the attributes needed to create the desired effects. Loading a brush simply changes the attributes.

Brushes can be used to create paint, as well as natural objects, hair, and other effects.

Strokes

When a brush is applied to the scene, it creates a curve known as a stroke. This curve is then used to define how the brush is rendered. Stroke curves are not to be confused with standard NURBS curves. Strokes contain additional data, such as tablet pressure. Paint Effects integrates nicely with pressure-sensitive graphics tablets. Almost any attribute in the Paint Effects interface can be affected by the pressure of the brush stroke.

Low qualities display less detail, but allow the scene to be manipulated more quickly.

If painting on a surface, the strokes can be offset so they're above or below the surface.

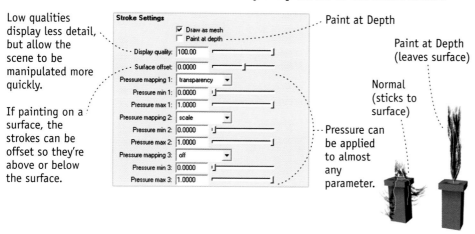

Paint at Depth

Paint at Depth (leaves surface)

Normal (sticks to surface)

Pressure can be applied to almost any parameter.

When Paint at Depth is on, the brush always paints at a fixed depth, set by the position of the cursor on the first click of the stroke, almost like a plane is placed at that depth for the duration of the stroke. This allows the stroke to leave the surface, such as for chimney smoke or water fountains.

The way strokes are painted is managed by the Paint Effects tool (choose Paint Effects → Paint Effects Tool).

Paint Effects allows you to paint strokes directly on NURBS or polygonal surfaces. This is great for adding grass to a ground plane, hair to a head, or feathers to a duck. When you paint directly on an object, Paint Effects creates a curve on the surface. This curve is locked to the geometry and moves and deforms with the object.

You can also paint on view planes. This allows you to paint strokes that are not connected to a specific piece of geometry, such as a cloud floating in the sky.

Paint Effects Window

While painting can be done in any 3D viewport, the Paint Effects window (choose Window →
Paint Effects) can offer increased performance, as well as the ability to blur and smear
brushes in 3D. It is also a place to create 2D paintings using Paint Effects's brush tools.

Main menu

Paint Chooses between
scene and canvas mode.

Camera Allows you to
choose a camera from the
scene.

Brush Allows you to choose
the brush and set options
such as Smear and Blur.

Resolution Helps speed
work flow on complex
scenes. It simply renders a
fraction of the pixel in the
scene, allowing for faster
screen updates.

Object Shading Chooses
between wireframe, shaded,
or textured, as well as
default or scene lighting.

Stroke Refresh When set
to Shade, it shows a fairly
accurate representation of
the final render.

Clear Canvas Deletes all the
strokes or clears the 2D
canvas.

Color Allows you to see the
RGB or Alpha channel.

Refresh Updates the display.

Flip Tubes Reverses direction
of tubes in relation to the
surface normals.

Brush settings These icons
change, depending on the
brush, and allow you to
modify such attributes as
color, transparency, and
tubes per step without
digging through an
Attributes panel.

Viewport In scene mode, the
window is 3D; in canvas
mode, 2D.

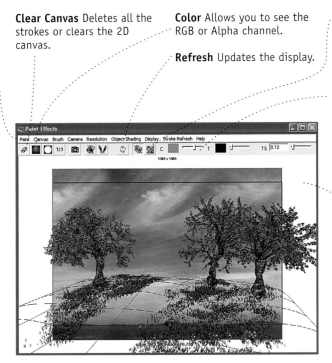

Scene Mode

Scene mode in the Paint Effects window works much like any 3D viewport, but it has a few
advantages. Brushes are fully rendered, and you can use tools such as Blur and Smear in
3D. It also gives you easy access to brush attributes such as color and transparency. This is
helpful for modifying brushes as you paint.

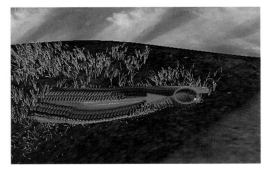

Unlike a 3D viewport (left), scene mode (right)
allows you to view rendered brushes in the viewport. Although this can take up resources, it's
much faster than doing test renders.

Scene mode also allows you to see effects such as
smear and blur, which are not shown in normal 3D
viewports.

Canvas Mode

Canvas mode does have limitations. Undo is limited to one level, and when painting, only the images are applied. Underlying strokes and brush attributes are discarded, so post-stroke editing is not possible.

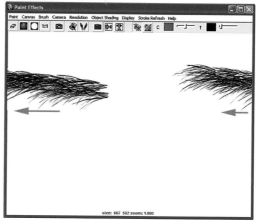

Canvas mode allows you to paint on a 2D canvas. This can be used to create entire paintings from scratch or to add paint effects to existing images. The Blur and Smear brushes are particularly useful in touching up existing images.

Another use for the window is in painting seamless textures. The canvas can wrap paintbrushes, so when they move off one edge of the canvas, they appear on the opposite edge. This is particularly useful when creating seamless textures.

Modifying Brushes

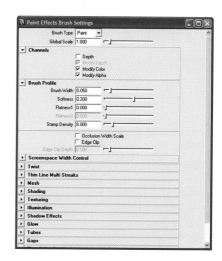

Painting with the supplied brushes can create some amazing effects, but the true power of Paint Effects shows itself when you create custom brushes. Understanding how brushes work goes a long way toward understanding how Paint Effects works.

When you create a brush, you can observe its attributes by pressing Ctrl+B to open the Brush Settings dialog box (choose Paint Effects → Template Brush Settings.) Here you can change a brush's behavior while you paint. Once the stroke is complete, the exact same set of attributes are located in the Attribute Editor, where you can change brushes that have already been painted.

> **TIP** When painting a fairly large surface, such as a field of grass, you will probably need to create several strokes to cover the area. If you need to change brush settings, such as the color or height of the grass, you normally have to change these values for every stroke. This is because Maya creates a new brush node for every new stroke. Toggling Share One Brush (choose Paint Effects → Share One Brush) allows you to paint many strokes, yet connect all of them to the same brush node. This makes editing easier, because you can edit one node, yet change many strokes.

Brush Types

When creating a brush, first consider the type of brush. Different brushes produce different effects as well as affect how a scene renders. Certain types of brushes also reveal different sets of attributes pertaining to that brush.

Paint: Applies paint to the canvas. Paintbrushes can create color as well as tubes and most other effects. They do not, however, create meshes, and some objects may break up when the camera gets close.

Smear: Distorts paint already applied.

Blur: Softens the look of the paint.

Erase: Removes the color from the painted pixels, revealing the underlying canvas.

Thin Line (bottom): Used to render large numbers of fine tubes much more quickly than the standard paintbrush (top). When used with the Multi Streak method, the Thin Line brush is much faster at creating hair than the standard paintbrush type and allows for effects such as wet hair.

Mesh: Renders Paint Effects using mesh-based tubes instead of brush stamps. This gives you much better control over textures and creates convincing close-ups of trees and plants. Generally, the Paintbrush tool is better when creating soft, fuzzy brushes, and the Mesh Brush tool is better at hard surfaces.

The difference between the results of using a mesh-type brush (right) and a paint-type brush (left) can be seen here. As the camera moves—compare the top images with the bottom—the mushrooms painted as a mesh change perspective, but those created as paint don't move properly. The paintbrush type is best used for objects that are less defined or don't change perspective.

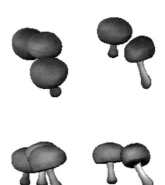

Brush Attributes

Paint Effects creates the illusion of solid paint by using a series of dots to represent splotches of paint. The closer the dots, the more solid the brush strokes appear. The basic brush attributes (found in the brush's Attribute Editor window) control the way the brush behaves as well as color and transparency.

Brush Profile controls the size and shape (left) of the brush as well as its softness (center). Stamp density (right) controls how solid or dotted the brush line paints.

Shading controls how the brush stroke is rendered. These controls are similar to the color controls in a material and affect (left to right) color, incandescence, and transparency.

Illumination allows the brush to appear 3D, much like a tube. The controls include settings for specularity and translucence. More important, this is where you control how the brush is lit, either from a user-defined lighting model or from real-world lights. Left, Specular Power; right, Specular Color.

Fractal   Checker   Ramp   Texture

Shadow Effects gives a brush the ability to cast shadows into the scene (center, a 2D shadow; right, a 3D shadow). Fake shadows work great for strokes on flat surfaces, and real shadows are good when the stroke needs to cast shadows on more complex geometry.

Texturing allows you to apply some procedural textures, such as ramps, checkers, and noise, along with a bitmap. Textures can also be applied to attributes such as transparency and displacement.

Tubes

In Paint Effects, a tube is an object that grows at angles from a stroke. If a brush containing tubes is painted on a surface, those tubes grow in the direction of the surface normals. If painted on a view plane, the direction of growth is specified by the user. Alone, tubes are good at simulating anything from grass to hair. By applying texture maps, you can even use tubes to simulate objects, such as mushrooms, rocks, or cities.

Tubes can get even more complex when they start branching. A simple tube can sprout branches, twigs, leaves, and flowers. Although these are primarily geared toward creating organic effects such as foliage, the same branching structures can be used for lightning, ice crystals, fire, and many other natural phenomena.

Basic Tube Attributes

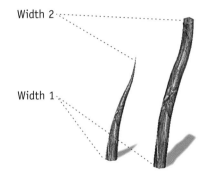

Width 2

Width 1

Tube creation attributes determine how many tubes are created and their density. Tubes Per Step determines how many tubes are created per stroke sample; this can be affected by a random amount. Here, Tubes Per Step is set at (left to right) 2, 12, and 48.

Tube Length: The range of lengths that the tubes will occupy. When creating grass, for example, the Length Min value is the shortest blade of grass, and Length Max is the longest.

Tube Width: These attributes determine the maximum diameter of the tubes. Tube1 determines the width at the base; Tube2, the tip.

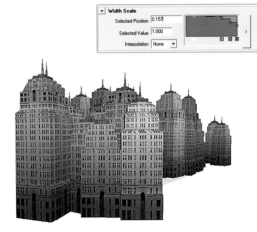

Width Scale: A ramp that can explicitly specify how a tube's width will change over its length. In this case, the stairstep outline of the buildings is created by defining a profile with the Width Scale ramp.

Tube Direction: This determines the direction in which the tubes will point. This can be along either the surface normals (left) or the direction of the path (right).

Growing and Branching

Tubes really show their power when they start growing and branching. Tubes can sprout tubes much like a tree trunk sprouts branches. These branches can, in turn, sprout twigs and leaves. Many objects and effects besides trees use branching structures, and one of the more powerful aspects of Paint Effects is the ability to generate these components in any way desired. A branching structure could just as easily be lightning flashing through the sky as a vine climbing on a wall.

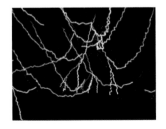

Growing a Tree

Paint Effects brushes can create incredibly complex objects. The sheer number of parameters can seem overwhelming. Even the most complex objects are built a step at a time, and if you break a complex object, such as a tree, into its component parts, it is much easier to understand.

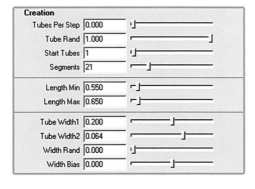

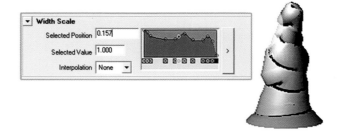

A tree always starts at the trunk, and Paint Effects starts with tubes. Here, we are creating a single tube for the trunk. The width parameters are adjusted so that the trunk is slightly wider at the base to create a conelike shape.

Tree trunks are seldom straight, and this trunk is no exception. To add some variation, the width of the tube is scaled using Width Scale. Anyone familiar with ramps will recognize the interface; a grayscale ramp defines variations in the width of the trunk.

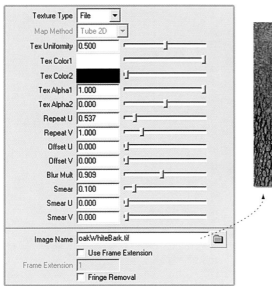

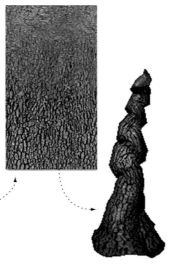

To add even more realism, color is added in the form of a photographic bitmap containing a tree bark texture. For a more stylized tree, you can draw or paint the texture and use that as a bitmap.

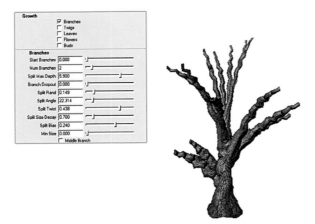

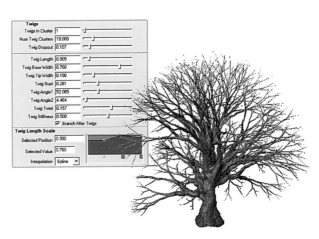

A tree always needs branches, so under Growth, branches are checked, and under Branches, the number of branches is configured.

Twigs are next and are simply branches of branches. Attributes to consider are the number of twigs, how much they twist, and their randomness, as well as a ramp that determines the length of the twigs.

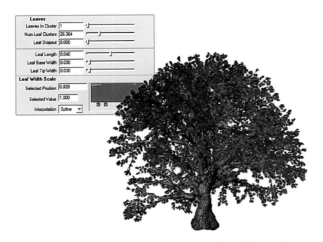

Leaves are next. Much like twigs, the size and number can be configured. Leaves can also be grouped in clusters. The width of the leaf can be set using a ramp. Additional attributes include the way the leaf curls and twists, as well as its stiffness.

Leaves also have color attributes. Simple color gradients can be applied, along with such parameters as specularity and translucence. For greater accuracy, a bitmap can be applied, such as this photographic leaf texture.

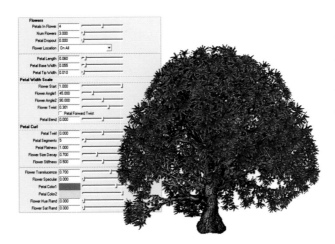

Flowers and buds can also be added. Flowers are similar to leaves, but instead of clustering, they can be arrayed radially in a series of petals. Attributes include the size and shape of the petals and the amount of curl and twist as well as color, which can include a bitmap. Buds are simply defined by the size of the bud and its color.

Painting a Scene

1 Choose File → Project → Set, navigate to the Chapter 7 folder on the companion CD, and set the current project to PaintFX. Load the scene Ch07_PaintFX_start.mb.

2 Using the perspective window, render the scene (choose Render → Render Current Frame). You should see a basic landscape with a sky in the background. Let's paint some foliage in the scene.

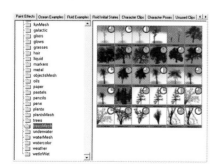

3 Select the ground plane (nurbsPlane1) as paintable (choose Paint Effects → Make

Paintable). Next, select a brush for painting. Open Visor (choose Window → General Editors → Visor), and, in the treesMesh folder, select Heavy Oak Tree.

4 In the perspective view, position the brush above the ground plane and paint a stroke to create an oak.

5 In the Outliner, you will see an object called strokeOakHeavy1. This is the brush stroke that generates the tree. Select this so we can manipulate the tree.

6 To make the tree larger, you can adjust the scale of the stroke in the Attribute Editor under the oakHeavy1 tab.

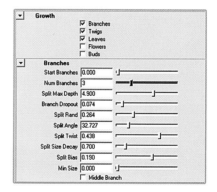

7 Other parameters can affect the shape, size, and color of the tree. Under the Tubes/Growth rollout, for example, we can change the number of branches, which affects the density of the foliage.

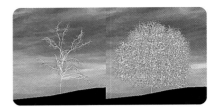

8 This shows the difference between one and three branches, respectively.

9 Let's add some grass. In the Visor window (choose Window → General Editors → Visor), select a grass brush.

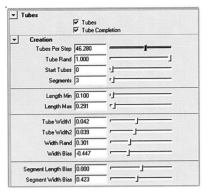

11 Select the stroke you just painted. In the Attribute Editor for the brush stroke, you can adjust the density of the grass by increasing or decreasing the strokes per step found under the Tubes/Creation rollout. This rollout also allows you to adjust the length, direction, and randomness of the grass.

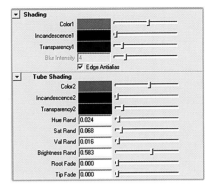

12 To change the color of the grass, modify the color of Tube Shading found under the Shading rollout.

10 Paint some grass along the ground plane.

13 Now that you have a basic understanding of the concepts, it's time to have fun. Add some more plants, grass, and trees as you see fit.

Deformations and Rigging

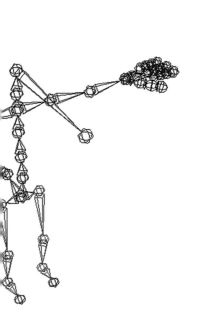

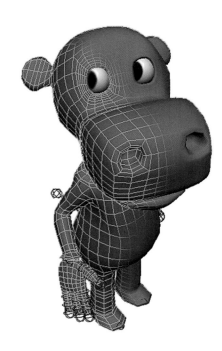

D eformations change the shape of an object. Almost any sort of organic animation—from a fully skinned character to flowers swaying in the breeze—will need deformations of one sort or another. In addition to using deformations for animation tasks, you can use them as modeling-tools. Since deformations can reshape a lot of detail quickly, deformers are good choices for global changes to an object.

Rigging is primarily used in character animation to create hierarchical structures called skeletons. Skeletons are used as a framework with which to deform the character as well as animate it. A good rig builds upon the skeleton to provide additional tools that make the animator's job easier by allowing the character to be quickly posed and manipulated.

8

131

Deformers

Basic deformations can be created using a class of tool called deformers. These are found in the Animation menu set under the Deform menu and work on any type of geometry. Maya deformers can be used as both an animation and a modeling tool.

Nonlinear Deformers

Nonlinear deformers (choose Deform → Create Nonlinear) can be used to quickly create a number of standard deformations and effects. You can use these for modeling, or you can animate the parameters. Each of these deformers can be adjusted from the Attributes panel or by using built-in manipulators. The effects are as follows.

Bend: Deforms the surface along an arc

Flare: Allows you to expand or contract the top or bottom of the object

Sine: Deforms the object based on a sine wave

Squash: Allows you to stretch or squash the object and still maintain its volume

Twist: Twists the object along an axis

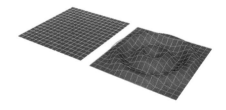

Wave: Deforms the object by using a circular wave

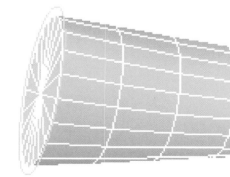

Clusters

Clusters (choose Deform → Create Cluster) are probably the simplest type of deformer, but they can also be useful. A cluster is simply a collection of points. When modeling, you can use clusters almost like selection sets to save collections of vertices. When animating, you can use clusters to fine-tune deformations or to create effects such as muscle bulging.

There are two main parameters to a cluster. *Envelope* is a falloff parameter used to create soft deformations. *Relative* is used to prevent double transformations when the vertices of the cluster are being controlled by another deformer.

You can weight clusters to give smooth falloffs. You can paint weights using the Paint Cluster Weights tool, or you can modify weights manually using the Component Editor.

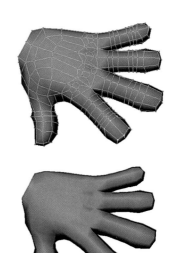

The vertices at the tip of this finger can be added to a cluster. Moving the cluster moves the vertices that constitute the cluster.

Soft Modification

Soft Modification (choose Deform → Soft Modification) is designed primarily as a modeling tool. It gives you the ability to push and pull geometry much like sculpting clay. Simply select the tool from the menu or from the Tool box, and then select a point on the surface. The Soft Modification tool appears, along with a manipulator that allows you to adjust the radius and falloff, which can also be adjusted using the tool's attributes.

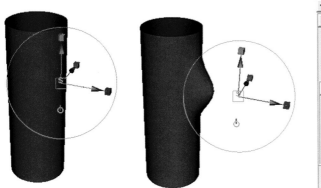
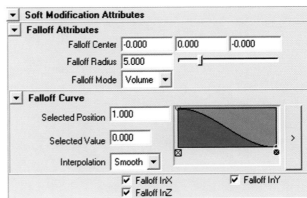

The Soft Modification tool's attributes can allow for custom falloff graphs.

Lattices

Lattice deformations (choose Deform → Create Lattice) use a three-dimensional grid of points as a way to deform an object. Changing the shape of the lattice changes the underlying object. Lattices are ideal for creating fairly large changes of a complex mesh, such as when the vertices are too close together for direct editing. You can use lattices as a modeling tool and, if the lattice is animated, as a deformation tool.

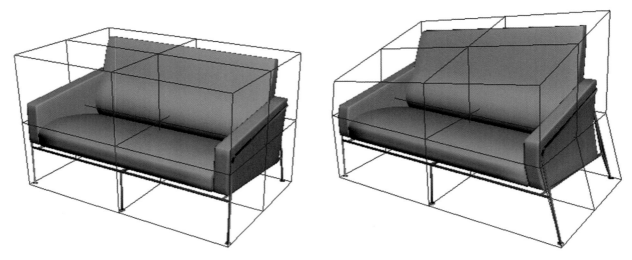

A lattice is a grid of points. When the lattice is deformed, the underlying mesh deforms along with it.

Lattices have controls to determine the number of points in each of the three dimensions. The trick to working with lattices is to use only enough detail to get the job done. Lattices are meant to simplify the deformation of an object, and having too many lattice points defeats the purpose.

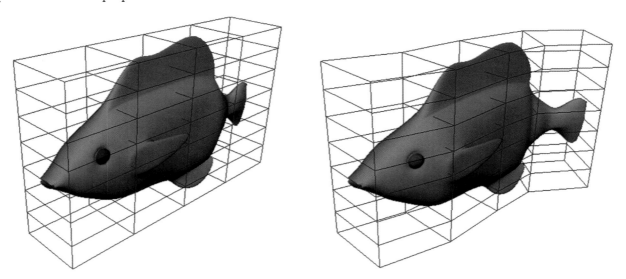

Lattices can also be used as an animation tool—for example, to make this fish deform so it can swim.

Sculpt Deformers

Not to be confused with the Sculpt Geometry tool, a sculpt deformer uses a tool called Influence Object to create bulging effects. Although this tool is normally spherical, a NURBS object can be used to manipulate the effect. Sculpt deformers can be used for a simple task, such as bulging a character's cheek, and for complex setups that mimic realistic muscles.

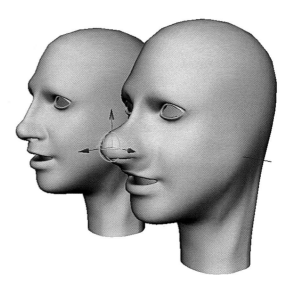

The mode determines how the tool works. Flip mode simply sticks the object's surface to the surface of the tool, so when the center of the tool passes through the object's surface, the surface snaps back. Project mode uses a projection to stick the object's surface onto the tool. Stretch mode stretches the object's surface to match that of the tool.

The maximum distance a vertex can be pushed.

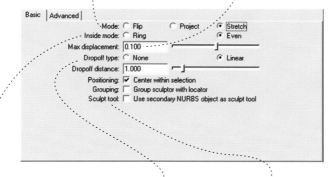

A sculpt deformer uses a NURBS object, such as this sphere, to create bulges in an object.

Determines how the vertices inside the sculpt sphere behave. Even creates a smooth deformation; Ring pushes the vertices to the outside of the sphere.

The falloff of the deformation. Linear sets a falloff, which can then be adjusted using the Dropoff Distance slider.

Allows you to add a secondary NURBS object as the deformer. This is used when creating advanced effects such as muscles.

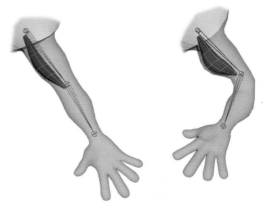

Sculpt deformers (left) can be used to simulate the realistic action of muscles (right). The muscle's shape is animated using a set driven key controlled by the angle of the elbow.

Sculpt deformer options

Wire Tool

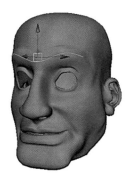

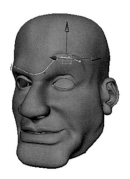

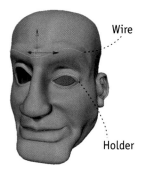

Moving the wire moves the underlying surface.

When you manipulate only part of the wire, you can smoothly deform parts of the model. The curves are usually animated using clusters or blend shapes.

The holder is a curve that limits the effect of the wire.

The Wire tool (choose Deform → Wire Tool) is similar to a sculpt deformer, but instead of using a NURBS surface to control the deformation, the Wire tool uses a simple NURBS curve. Manipulating the curve moves the underlying surface within the falloff distance.

The process for creating a wire deformer is a little bit different from the process for creating most deformers in that you first select the tool, then the deformed surface, and finally the wire.

At times, a wire curve's influence can affect unwanted parts of the model. You can prevent this using a holder to limit the effect of the wire. Those parts of the model on the other side of the holder will not deform.

Wrap Deformers

A wrap deformer allows a low-resolution mesh to deform a more-complex model. This is particularly useful in character animation, in which low-resolution meshes are employed to speed animation authoring and playback, but high-resolution meshes are needed for rendering. Wraps can be computationally expensive, however, and wrapped objects may have to be placed on layers and hidden to speed work flow.

Wraps are easy to apply. Simply select the objects to be wrapped, then select the wrapper, and choose Deform → Create Wrap. The real trick with wraps is to create a good wrapper. This can entail creating an entirely new model just as the wrap. In the case of a

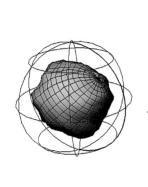

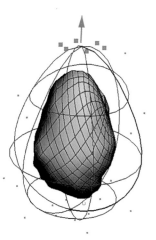

Wrap deformers allow a low-res object to control a more-complex one.

polygonal model, a wrapper can be created from the original low-res version of the complex model. In the case of a NURBS model, you have to model a polygonal cage, paying attention to where the detail on the NURBS surface lies.

Jiggle Deformers

Primarily used in animation, a jiggle deformer (choose Deform → Create Jiggle Deformer) automatically moves the affected surface points to create a jiggle motion as the object moves. This is great for creating secondary motion in character animation to simulate such motions as a jiggling belly.

Since the Jiggle Deformer tool can be resource intensive, Maya offers an option to cache the motion (choose Deform → Create Jiggle Disk Cache) for faster work flows. Once the cache is created, subsequent playbacks happen much closer to real-time. Additionally, when jiggle animation needs to be rendered with motion blur, you must create jiggle disk cache.

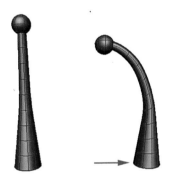

Jiggle deformers create automatic secondary motion.

There are several attributes to consider when setting up a jiggle deformer. Stiffness, Damping, and Jiggle Weight control the amount of jiggle effect, and Force Along Normal, Force On Tangent, and Direction Bias control the direction of the jiggle.

Blend Shapes

Blend shapes, also known as morph targets, allow you to change the shape of one object to match another. This is a precise way to deform an object, as each target of the blend shape can be modeled using Maya's modeling tools. Blend shapes can also combine multiple targets to mix and match deformations.

The big task in creating a blend shape is creating the targets. This is primarily a modeling task. The one requirement for blend shape targets is that they all have the same topology as the base object. This is easily accomplished by duplicating the base object (such as a head) and reshaping it to create the appropriate shape (such as a blink or a smile.)

Once the targets are created, setting up the blend shape is simply a matter of selecting all the targets first, the base model last, and choosing Deform → Create Blend Shape. Once the blend shape is created, the resulting shapes can be mixed using the Blend Shape Editor (choose Window → Animation Editors → Blend Shape).

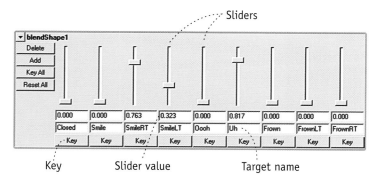

The Blend Shape Editor allows you to mix multiple targets. Each channel has a slider and a Key button, as well as a box for the slider value. By default, sliders go from 0 to 1, but you can type any number into the slider value field to push a slider past its limit or make it go negative.

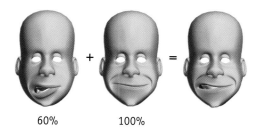

60%   100%

Blend shapes allow you to mix different shapes to create a new result.

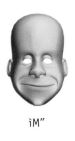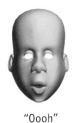

"M"   "Oooh"   "Oh"   "E" and consonants

Blend shapes called phonemes can be created to mimic the basic mouth positions used in dialogue.

"A" and "I"   "Eh" and "Uh"   "F" and "V"   "L" and "Th"

Blend shapes work by averaging the X, Y, and Z positions of each individual vertex or CV in the object. When a slider is at 0%, the vertex is at the rest position; at 100%, it is at the target. Mixing multiple targets averages the positions according to the weights on the sliders.

Although blend shapes can be used for any type of shape animation, by far the most popular application for blend shapes is in facial animation. A modeler creates individual facial poses representing the extreme motions of the individual parts of the face, such as smiling or opening the jaw. By mixing these, you can create an infinite variety of facial expressions.

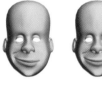

Other blend shapes can be modeled for positions the mouth makes when not speaking, such as a smile. It's always a good idea to create right and left versions of these shapes so that the animator can create asymmetry in the facial expressions.

Shapes for the upper part of the face include blinks and brow positions for emotions such as worry, anger, and surprise. Again, it is a good idea to create left and right versions of these shapes to give the animator more control.

Skeletons and Rigging

Skeletons in Maya are constructed from objects called joints. These joints are tied together in a hierarchy. The skeleton, in turn, is used to deform a mesh using Maya's skinning tools. Although skeletons are used primarily for character animation, they can also be used to deform all sorts of other deformations. A garden hose, for example, can easily be deformed using a series of joints. Joints can also help refine the behavior of hair and clothing.

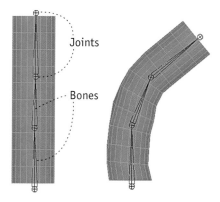

Joints are used to guide deformations using the skinning tools. When the joints move, the mesh deforms to match. The joint is the actual axis of rotation, and the bones span the joints.

When building a skeleton, it is always a good idea to study the anatomy of the character or creature you are rigging. Getting the skeleton anatomically correct will make the resulting deformations anatomically correct as well. The joints of this character closely mimic the joints of a real skeleton.

Basics of Joints

Joints are created using the Joint tool (choose Skeleton → Joint Tool), which is also available on the Animation shelf. Choosing the tools allows you to sketch out the joints, almost like drawing a curve, with one joint being created per LMB click.

> **TIP** To add to a skeleton, highlight a joint in the skeleton, choose the Joint tool, and start drawing joints. The new joints become children of the highlighted joint. You can also connect existing joints by choosing Skeleton → Connect Joint.

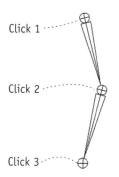

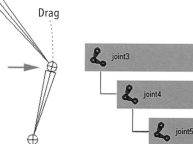

Creating joints is as simple as drawing them using the LMB. Each click creates a joint.

Modifying joints is fairly easy, as you can simply select the joint and move it to precisely position it.

When a skeleton is drawn, the joints automatically form a hierarchy.

Joint Attributes

Each joint has an array of attributes to control how it behaves when manipulated and animated. The basic attributes control the joint's position and rotation, but there are additional attributes.

Draws the resulting joint as a bone or a box.

The translation, rotation, and scale of the joint.

Used in Inverse Kinematics to determine the rest position of a joint.

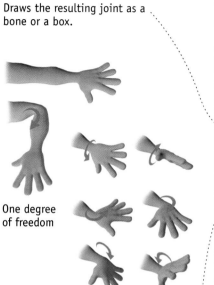

One degree of freedom

Three degrees of freedom

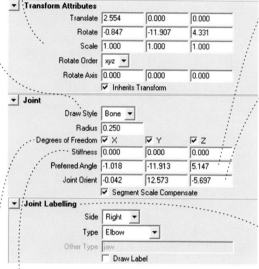

Determines how the joints are oriented with respect to each other.

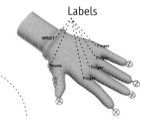

Labels

Limiting the degrees of freedom limits how the joint will rotate. A neck or wrist joint usually has three degrees of freedom, and a knee or an elbow has only one.

The stiffness of a joint comes into play when Inverse Kinematics (IK) is applied. Stiffer joints resist motion, so they rotate less when IK solutions are calculated.

Joints can have labels applied to them, making them easier to identify in a complex rig.

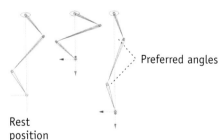

Preferred angles

Rest position

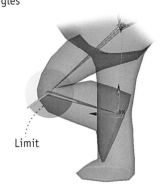

Limit

Joints can also be limited in their range of motion. Limiting the motion at the joint to limits found in nature also keeps the character's motion natural when animated.

A knee, for example, rotates through only about 100–120 degrees.

Inverse Kinematics

By default, joints in Maya move strictly by rotation. This is called *Forward Kinematics* (FK), because a series of joints is manipulated from the root joint forward. If a character picks up a cup of coffee, the joints are posed starting at the shoulder and forward to the fingertips. Forward Kinematics is great for most motions, but it can pose a serious problem whenever a character needs to keep one part of the body stable while the other moves, such as keeping a foot on the ground during a walk or a run.

To overcome this limitation, Inverse Kinematics (IK) can be used. Inverse Kinematics automatically rotates a chain of joints so that the end points can be positioned using translation instead of rotation. This is perfect for a character's legs, but also can be used in other areas, such as arms. If a character climbs a ladder, for example, the hands have to remain stable on the rungs while the shoulders move.

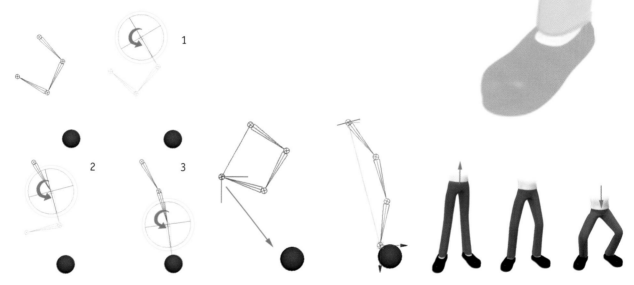

To get the end of this joint chain to reach the ball using Forward Kinematics, all joints in the chain need to be rotated, requiring several steps.

Inverse Kinematics allows you to position the joints simply by translating the IK handle to the desired location, using one step. The IK Solver rotates the joints automatically.

A character's legs are a perfect place to use IK because it allows the hips to move freely while the feet remain firmly planted on the ground.

TIP   Joint flipping is an unwanted effect that happens when the end effector of the chain is moved past the pole of the chain. At this point, the IK solution crosses over 360 degrees, flipping the joints. To offset this, you can animate the pole vector of the chain away from the end effector to avoid flipping.

Configuring IK

To set up IK, choose Skeleton → IK Handle Tool, and then select the start and end joints of the IK chain. Selecting the IK handle lets you control the attributes and behavior of the chain, using the IK Attributes panel.

Snaps the IK handle back to the end of the joint; useful when switching from IK to FK and back.

Used when creating overlapping IK chains; allows one handle to take priority over others in case of a conflict.

Used with multiple IK chains; allows the chain's priority to be weighted.

Maya provides two different ways for an IK chain to be solved, allowing for slightly different behaviors.

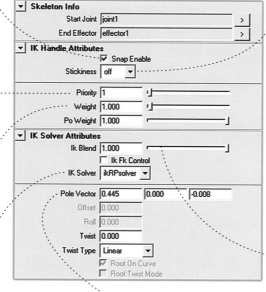

When stickiness is enabled, movement of the start joint does not affect the end effector (center object is set to Sticky, right is Off). Sticky is desirable for a character's legs, where the hips need to move while the feet remain stable.

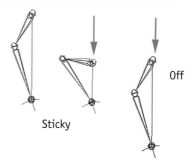

Off

Sticky

Used when switching from IK to FK and back. If IK is simply toggled on or off, it can cause the animation to "pop." Blending allows you to gradually turn on the IK handle, allowing for a smoother transition from IK to FK and back.

Determines the position of the pole vector; useful in preventing joint flipping.

Reference plane

Joint chain plane

Handle vector

Handle

Single Chain Solver The simplest solver, it rotates the joints so that they all lie along a fixed plane. Good for simple joints that have only one degree of freedom, such as a knee.

Rotate Plane Solver Adds a second parameter to allow you to use a manipulator to rotate the chain around an axis. Useful for joints such as elbows, which can be rotated to many positions, even though the ends of the chain (shoulder and wrist) are in fixed positions.

Spline IK

Another way to configure IK is by using Spline IK, which employs a curve to control the joints and their rotations. This is a good choice for manipulating long chains, such as a tail, a trunk, or even a spine.

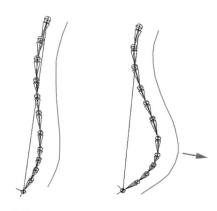

Spline IK works best with chains that have a lot of short bones. To create a Spline IK chain, choose Skeleton → IK Spline Handle Tool, and then choose the start and end joints in the chain. Maya automatically generates a curve to fit the chain. You can modify the resolution of the curve as the chain is created using the tool's options.

Spline IK uses a NURBS curve to control the shape of a joint chain.

Once created, the Spline IK curve is like any other NURBS curve and can be animated using clusters or blend shapes.

Spring IK Solver

Spring IK rotates bone chains proportionally across all affected joints. You can specify a bias that ensures the angles between the joints are evenly distributed. Spring Solvers require a rest pose. If the handle is moved, then the distance between the handle and the rest position of the handle determines whether the chain is extended or flexed. Spring IKs are typically used for numerous-joint chains, such as insect legs.

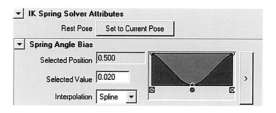 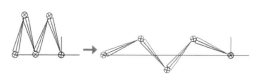

A spring IK handle is moved to extend the skeleton. The joint rotations are evenly distributed, with an added bias.

Full-Body IK

In the past, separate IK chains were created manually throughout the character and did not have any relationship with one another. Maya's full-body Inverse Kinematics system automates much of the IK creation and consolidates their functionality into a single full-body IK Solver.

This full-body solver sets relationships between all of the IK chains so that if a character moves his arm outward, the rest of his body will translate and rotate along with it. This automated movement can create very realistic and easy-to-set-up animation.

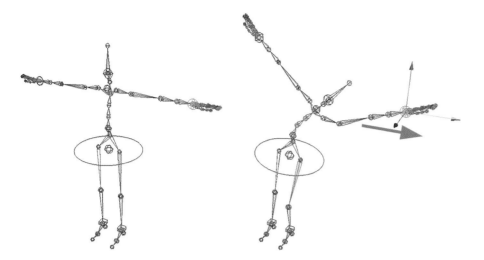

(left) This skeleton shows the full-body IK set up on a skeleton in the standard T-pose. (right) As the skeleton's left arm is translated down the X axis, notice how the rest of the body pulls with it.

Although it can be very nice to have automated secondary motion when moving various IK handles around, sometimes you need to pin an effector. For instance, if you are posing your character's foot up on an object, you do not want it to leave if you change the location or rotation of another effector.

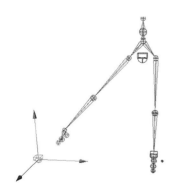

The hips are pinned in this skeleton, so only the right leg follows the effector's location.

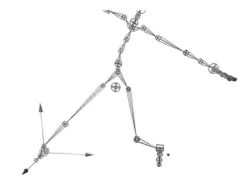

There is no pinning in this skeleton, so the whole body conforms to the right foot's extreme position.

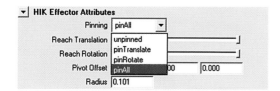

You can choose to pin the translation, rotation, or both for each effector in the full-body IK Solver.

Constraints

Constraints are a way to automatically control an object's position, scale, or orientation. Constraints are used in animation as well as in character rigging to provide animators with ways to attach parts of a character's body to other objects or parts of a scene.

Point

In animation, a point constraint causes one object to move to and follow the position of another object, or the average position of several objects. Point constraints are particularly useful when you want an object to match another object's position while keeping it outside the hierarchy, such as when a character is lifting something.

When the character lifts the ball, the ball is constrained to the palm of the hand. This allows the ball to move with the hand as the hand itself is animated.

Aim

An aim constraint constrains an object's orientation so that the object aims at other objects. In character setup, a typical use of an aim constraint is to set up a locator that controls eyeball movement.

The eyeball is aim-constrained to the locator and rotates to follow it.

Pole Vector

A pole vector constraint causes an IK chain's pole vector to move to and follow the position of an object. This is useful for preventing joint flipping and can be used to create a helper object used in positioning joints such as knees.

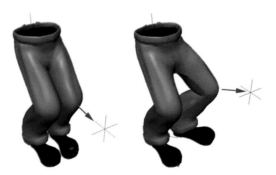

A pole vector constraint and an IK chain's pole vector, allowing directional control of the solver plane

Multiple Constraints and Constraint Weights

Constraints can be weighted to allow objects to attach and detach themselves from other objects, such as when a character is lifting an object. You can also apply multiple constraints to allow an object to switch from one object to another (such as when a character is moving an object from one hand to another) or to keep an object between two other objects.

pSphere1_pointConstrai	
Node State	Normal
Offset X	0
Offset Y	0
Offset Z	0
P Cube1 W0	1
P Cube2 W1	1

The sphere is constrained to both cubes; so when one cube is moved, the sphere remains centered between them.

In the Channel Box, the constraint's node contains a weight for each constrained object (here, P Cube1 W0 and P Cube2 W1). When a weight is zero, the constraint has no effect. Adjusting the weights allows the object to favor one object over another.

Skinning

Skeletons provide the structure of the body, but the skin provides the appearance. Getting the mesh of the character to deform according to the position of the character's skeleton is called skinning. Most characters animated in Maya will be skinned in some form, and getting a character's mesh to deform smoothly usually takes a good knowledge of the skinning tools and how they work. Maya has two features for skinning characters, Rigid Bind and Smooth Bind. These tools work slightly differently, and each has advantages.

Rigid Bind

Rigid Bind (choose Skin → Bind Skin → Rigid Bind) breaks each part of the surface into clusters and associates each cluster with a joint. This type of binding does not allow for the weighting of vertices across multiple joints.

   To compensate for the lack of weighting, Rigid Bind incorporates a number of tools called flexors that allow for control over the joints. Flexors are attached to the joint or the bone and can be used to fine-tune the bending and creasing of a joint or to create other effects, such as muscle bulging.

Lattice Flexors

These surround the mesh with a user-defined lattice that is centered on the joint's rotation axis. The lattice's attributes contain some predefined behaviors.

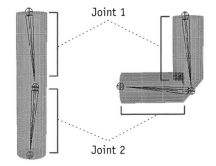

By default, Rigid Bind assigns each part of the mesh to only one joint.

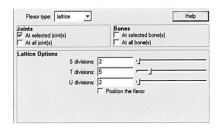

Create Flexor options

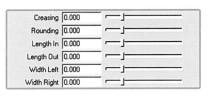

Lattice flexor attributes

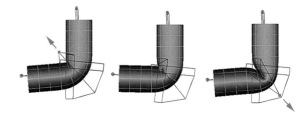

Creasing determines the amount of crease on the inside of the bend.

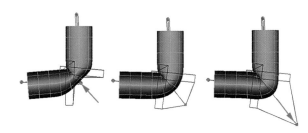

Rounding determines the bulge at the "elbow" of the joint.

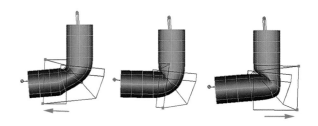

Length In/Out allows sliding of the skin over the joint.

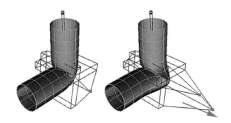

Width Left/Right allows the skin in the joint area to squash outward or inward to help preserve volume.

Sculpt Flexors

Sculpt flexors apply a sculpt deformer and center it on the joint. Sculpt flexors can be used to create muscle bulges based on joint angle. To do so, create a set driven key for the sculpt deformer and drive it by the angle of the joint.

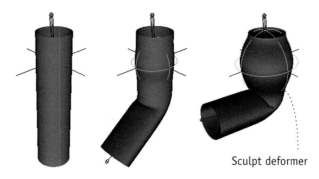

Sculpt deformer

Sculpt flexors use a sculpt deformer to modify the appearance of the skin.

Joint Cluster Flexors

These create a cluster representing the vertices affected by the joint. This allows for weighted deformations, and joint clusters are differentiated from regular clusters by using the letter *J*.

> **TIP** When modifying joint weights or flexors, it's a good idea to animate the joint into its extreme positions before modifying the weights. This way, instead of selecting and deselecting the joint and moving it to test a deformation, you can simply drag the Time slider to move the joint.

Joint clusters allow for weighting, and when the Manipulator tool is used, the shape of the joint's deformation can be adjusted.

Smooth Bind

Smooth Bind (choose Skin → Bind Skin → Smooth Bind) is the second and more widely used type of skinning. It creates good results without the need for flexors and deformers to control deformation at the joints. Smooth Bind works by allowing individual vertices to be weighted across multiple joints. This allows each vertex to be controlled by multiple joints, providing a smooth transition from one joint to another. It does not allow for effects such as muscle bulges and creases, but you can add these by using standard Maya deformers.

Once the skin is bound to the skeleton using Smooth Bind, you can edit weights using either the Component Editor or the Paint Weights tool. The general work flow is to use the Paint Skin Weights tool for the global changes and then fine-tune problem areas a vertex at a time using the Component Editor.

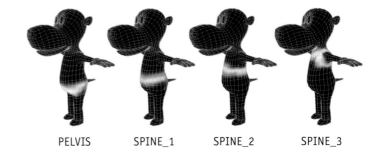

PELVIS   SPINE_1   SPINE_2   SPINE_3

Smooth Bind weighting for a simple character. The gray areas are where the weighting overlaps.

Paint Skin Weights

Painting weights is the most interactive way to adjust the weighting of a smoothly bound skin. The interface uses the standard Artisan tools to paint the weight maps. You can access the Paint Skin Weights tool by choosing Skin → Edit Smooth Skin → Paint Skin Weights Tool.

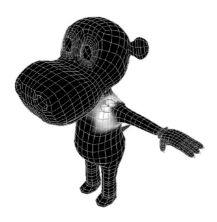

When painting weights, the affected vertices show up as white or gray; unaffected vertices show up black.

Turn on Multi-color Feedback in the Paint Skin Weights tool's Display options. The colors on the bound geometry correspond to the weight of a bone with a matching color.

Options to control the size and shape of the brush.

The current joint is selected using the list or by RMB-clicking over the joint in the viewport.

Forces all weights on the current joint to be held at their current weight, allowing you to paint other joints without affecting the "held" joint.

Changes the behavior of the brush to allow you to replace current weights, as well as scale, add, or smooth the weights.

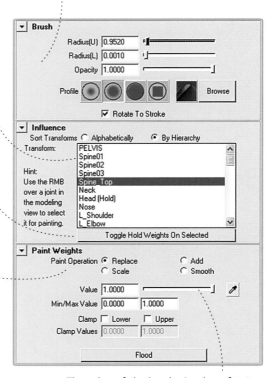

The value of the brush. A value of 1.0 fully weights the vertex to the joint.

The Paint Skin Weights tool

Component Editor

The Component Editor (choose Window → General Editors → Component Editor) allows you to affect the weighting of each individual vertex. To use the editor, select a vertex or a group of vertices on the object, and these will show up in the Component Editor. The weights of each vertex are displayed on a per vertex basis.

TIP Sometimes a vertex is affected by many joints. This can cause unwanted deformations and slow performance. Choosing Skin → Edit Smooth Skin → Prune Small Weights can get rid of the unwanted influences.

Selected vertices

For a complex skin, most of the weights for a set of vertices will be zero. To see just the affected joints for those vertices, choose Options → Hide Zero Columns.

Weights Each vertex has a weight for each joint. The total of all weights must never be greater than 1. You can type weights into individual cells or select multiple cells for global changes.

The Component Editor has tabs for a number of Maya features. To edit weights for a skinned object, select Smooth Skins.

To use the Component Editor, select the vertices to be modified, and then open the Component Editor (choose Window → General Editors → Component Editor).

Hold Similar to Toggle Hold in the Paint Skin Weights tool, it allows you to hold the current weight values of that joint while other weights are edited.

Joints are listed in columns.

Vertices are listed in rows.

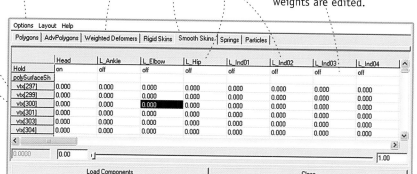

The Component Editor

Mirroring or Copying Weights

Most characters are fairly symmetrical, so you can fine-tune the skin on one side of your character and simply mirror those weights to the other half. To do so, choose Skin → Edit Smooth Skin → Mirror Skin Weights. The mirror axis is specified in the tool's options. For mirroring to work, the character's pivot needs to be centered along the left/right axis of the character.

Maya also offers a way to copy weights from one character to another. The weighting is copied based on the relative positions of the vertices compared to the joints. It should give a good first pass when skinning similar characters, leaving just minor cleanup.

Creating a Skeleton

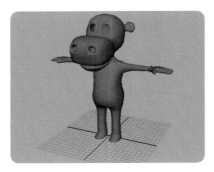

1 Open the file
Ch08_Skel_Start.mb. This
contains the character created in
Chapter 3.

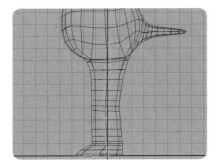

2 In the side viewport, use the
Joint tool (choose Skeleton →
Joint Tool) to draw three bones
representing the thigh, shin, and
foot.

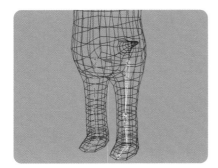

3 In the perspective viewport,
highlight the chain by clicking
the root joint and move it to position it in the middle of the left leg.
Duplicate this chain (choose Edit →
Duplicate) to make the right leg
skeleton.

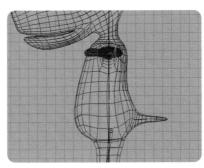

4 In the side viewport, create a
four-joint spine. Follow the
general outline of the back of the
character.

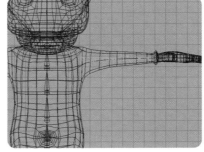

5 In the front viewport, draw the
left arm skeleton consisting of a
shoulder, bicep, and forearm. Make
sure the shoulder joint ends slightly
to the outside of the armpit. Check
the positioning of these joints in the
top viewport to make sure they are
centered in the arm.

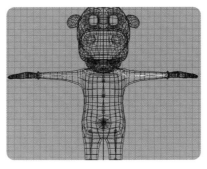

6 Select the root joint of the left
arm and mirror this (choose
Skeleton → Mirror Joint) across the
YZ axis to create the right arm.

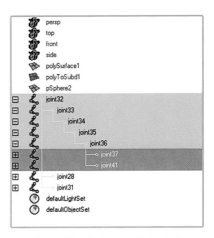

7 Open the Outliner. Select the
spine hierarchy and expand it.
MMB and drag the root joints of the
arms to the top of the spine. MMB
and drag the root joints of the legs
to the base of the spine.

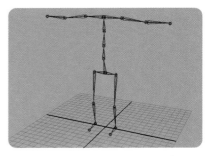

8 Dragging the joints into the
hierarchy creates new bones at
the pelvis and clavicle.

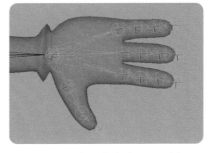

9 Create a hand skeleton with
three joints for each finger, all
connected to the arm at the wrist.
Mirror this to create the opposite
hand.

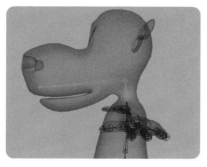

10 Create a neck joint and one large joint for the head.

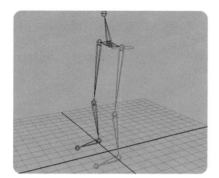

11 Create an IK chain for each leg. Choose Skeleton → IK Handle Tool, and then select the root of the left leg (at the hip) and the left ankle. Repeat this for the right leg.

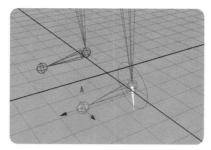

12 To maintain control of the foot, create an IK handle between the ankle and the toe on each leg. This will allow the foot to point at the IK handle rather than rotate with the ankle joint.

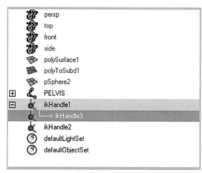

13 Select the IK handle of the toe, and make it the child of the leg's IK handle. This will allow you to move the entire foot by grabbing the ankle, and change the angle of the foot by adjusting the handle at the toe.

14 The completed skeleton is ready for skinning.

Skinning a Character

Properly skinning a character is a detailed process. It involves testing the character over a wide range of motions and making sure all the vertices deform properly. This tutorial gives you the broad strokes; the detail work is up to you.

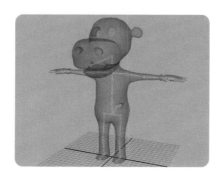

1 Open the file Ch08_Skin_Start.mb. Apply a smooth skin by choosing the root of the skeleton and then the skin of the character. Choose Skin → Bind Skin → Smooth Bind.

2 Start refining the weighting. In this case, we'll start with the head. To make the work flow easier, create a small test animation of the head and neck going through the range of motions—up and down, right and left.

3 Select the mesh, and start the weighting by using the Paint Skin Weights tool (choose Skin → Edit Smooth Skin → Paint Skin Weights Tool). Select the head joint, and paint the weights of the head completely white.

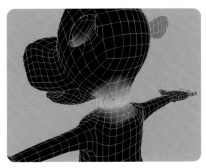

4 Select the neck and paint a transition (gray) from the head

to the neck, and from the neck to the top of the spine. Use the Time slider to check the deformation to make sure it is reasonably smooth. Check for any stray deformations on the body, and paint those black.

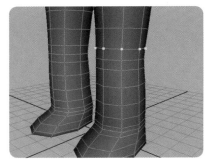

5 Now let's use the Component Editor to adjust some of the weighting around the legs. First, move the IK handle on the left leg and create some keyframes to get the legs moving.

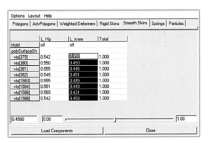

6 There are three rows of vertices around the knee. Select the vertices in the topmost of these rows.

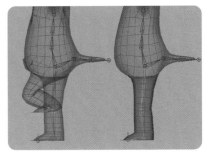

7 Open the Component Editor (choose Window → General Editors → Component Editor). Under Options, choose Hide Zero Columns. This should just show the

weights for the two joints affecting the knee vertices (L_Knee, L_Hip). Select the weights, and adjust them so that row of vertices deforms smoothly.

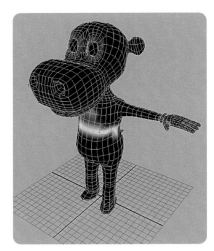

8 Test the deformation by scrubbing the Time slider. Adjust the rest of the knee vertices in the same manner.

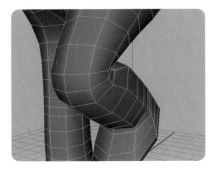

9 Now you have a basic understanding of the two tools used to weight the skin. The rest is just detail work. Take your time and finish the character, using the Paint Skin Weights tool for global changes and the Component Editor for detail work. To save time, work on just the left half first, and then use Mirror Skin Weights to copy the weighting to the other side.

Animation

So far, we've been working in the three dimensions of space. Time adds a dimension to your work. Changing an object over time is called animation, and animation is what truly brings your scene to life. The way an object moves tells the audience a lot about its size and weight and, for a character, its personality.

Maya has a wealth of tools for creating and sculpting motion. Learning how to use the tools, though, is only the first step in the process. An animator must understand how the laws of motion work, as well as how the audience perceives motion. Character animators also have to learn how motion affects a character's personality and mood.

Creating Animation

Maya offers a variety of methods for creating animation. Each method has its advantages. Understanding each method will let you decide which approach to take when animating a scene.

Creating keys (choose Animate → Set Key) is the most common way of animating within Maya. A key simply records an attribute's value at a given point in time. By changing the value over time, you create motion and animation. Keys allow you a wide degree of control over every attribute of an object, from its position to color and just about everything else. To edit keys, you use the Graph Editor and the Dope Sheet. Both allow you to control timing precisely.

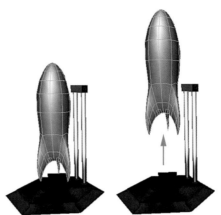

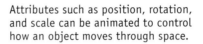
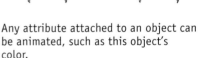

Attributes such as position, rotation, and scale can be animated to control how an object moves through space.

Any attribute attached to an object can be animated, such as this object's color.

Path Animation

Path animation (choose Animate → Motion Paths) allows you to draw out a path that the object will take through the scene. Path animation is used a lot when animating vehicles, but can be used almost any time an object needs to follow a specific route through the scene.

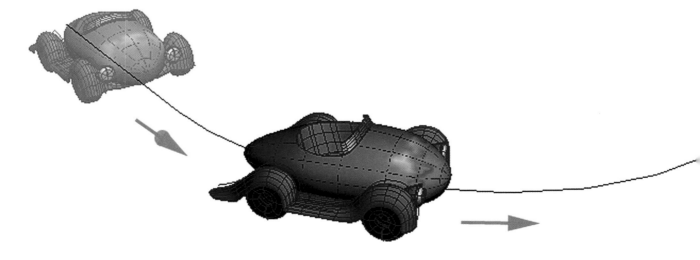

Set Driven Keys

Set driven keys allow you to let the motion of one object drive another. Set driven keys are used extensively in character rigging to make a character easy to animate. A blend shape that controls a character's jaw, for example, can drive the motion of the teeth.

Set driven keys are also used with custom attributes to create single points of control for a character. Controls for a character's fingers might be ties to custom attributes on the wrist, for example. This allows the animator to select one object and control the entire hand.

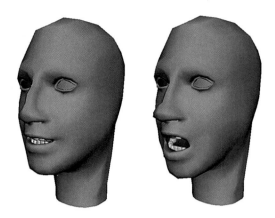

The teeth on this character are animated using a set driven key. As the jaw opens, the teeth move to match.

Nonlinear Animation

Nonlinear animation uses Maya's Trax Editor to combine animation clips to build animation a motion at a time rather than a key at a time. Clips can be trimmed, stretched, cycled, and blended together to create entirely new motions. Nonlinear animation is used a lot in character animation, but has uses in many other places.

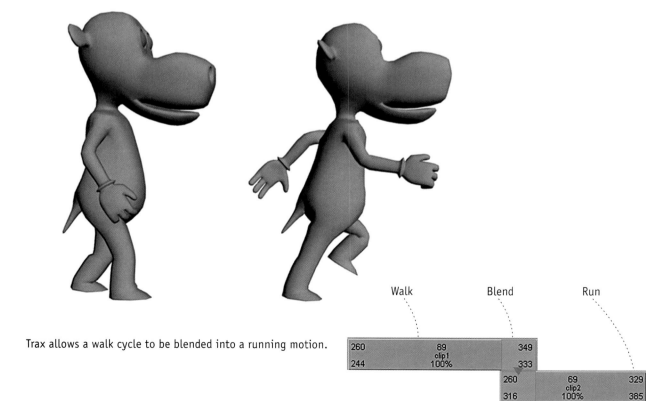

Trax allows a walk cycle to be blended into a running motion.

Expressions

Expressions are mathematical equations, programming commands, and MEL (Maya Embedded Language) commands that can precisely control an object's motion. Expressions are used a lot in rigging, but can also be used to create motion that follows mathematical equations. For example, an expression can rotate the tires on a car according to distance traveled.

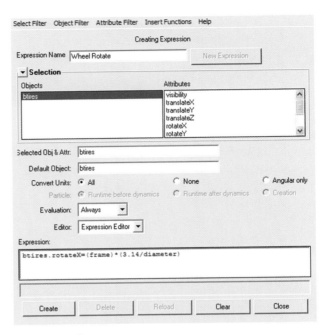

Expression Editor

Motion of car

Rotation calculated by expression

Simulations

Simulating the laws of nature can also create animation. Maya's Soft and Rigid Body dynamics let you set up an initial set of conditions, apply forces such as wind and gravity, and run the simulation. This type of animation is particularly useful when creating special effects.

Creating Keys

In Maya, time is defined by keys, which record attribute changes over time. Almost anything in Maya can be animated, from an object's position in space to its shape and color.

You can set keys in many ways within Maya. Which method you choose depends on the attributes being animated and the tool that is most convenient at the time.

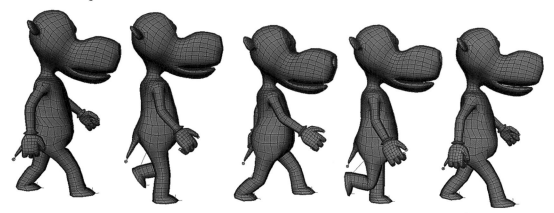

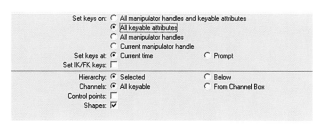

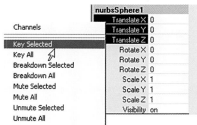

Set Key: Keys can be set by choosing Animate → Set Key, which sets keyframes on the selected objects. This option sets keys for all keyable attributes.

Channel box: Right-clicking in the Channel box opens a menu that contains options to set a key for all the channels or just those currently selected.

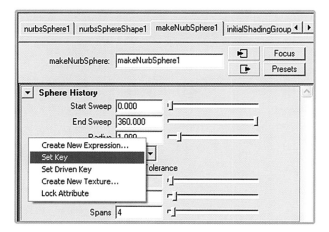

Attribute Editor: Right-clicking over an attribute in the Attribute Editor opens a menu from which you can set a key. This method is good for keying attributes that do not appear in the Channel box.

Auto Key: Setting a lot of keys can get tedious, so Maya provides an Auto Key function, which can be turned on by toggling the icon with a key on it to the right of the Timeline.

Keyboard shortcuts: Pressing S sets a key for all keyable attributes on the selected objects. Holding the Shift key and pressing W, E, or R, keys position, rotation, and scale, respectively.

Working with the Time Slider

The Time slider allows you to move quickly from one frame to the next in order to set keyframes or scrub through your animation. The slider is a horizontal bar, divided into frames.

Keys Each key in the Timeline shows up as a vertical red tick at the keyed frame.

Sound Sound is imported into Maya. You can then display it by right-clicking in the Time slider and choosing sounds from the menu. Visualizing the sound against your keys helps the animation process.

Selecting keys Shift+click and drag to select multiple keys. You can then drag these along the Timeline. Dragging the arrows stretches or compresses the animation.

Current frame

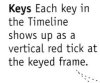
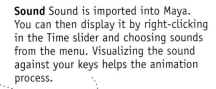

Start frame First frame of the animation.

Range start First frame of the current range.

Time range This bar allows you to see a smaller portion of a scene, which is helpful when working with large scenes. Dragging the ends shows more or less of the animation; dragging the middle moves the range.

Range end

End frame

Playing Animation

Once keyframes for a particular scene are set, you can play back the animation. You can play back directly in a viewport simply by clicking the Play button, located toward the bottom-right corner of the Maya interface. You can play back forward and backward.

Play

Next key

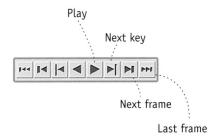

Next frame

Last frame

Playblast

Even on the fastest workstation, complex scenes often do not play back in a viewport in real time. This is when you need to use Maya's Playblast feature (choose Window → Playblast), which steps through the animation and renders to disk a small movie file that actually can be played back in real time.

Viewer The viewer can be either a movie player (QuickTime or Windows) or Maya's own FCheck format.

Time Range The range of the animation to be played back.

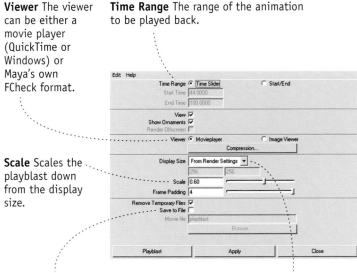

Scale Scales the playblast down from the display size.

Save To File Playblasts can be saved for later review.

Display Size Sets the size of the playblast, either from the viewport size or the size of the rendered image in the Render Globals window.

Editing Animation

Keys can be edited to fine-tune the look and feel of the scene. Simple editing can be done on the Timeline by selecting and moving keys. For more-complex editing, use the Graph Editor and the Dope Sheet.

Dope Sheet

The Dope Sheet (choose Window → Animation Editors → Dope Sheet) presents animation as keys set against a timeline. This window is used primarily to adjust and set timing.

Keys are displayed in the Outliner pane on the left side of the Dope Sheet window. LM-click to select keys.

You can move keys individually, in groups, or hierarchically. To move keys, select the Move tool (shortcut key W), MM-click, and drag the selected keys.

TIP **Right-clicking in the view area of the Dope Sheet opens a menu that allows you to cut and paste keys as well as apply curve filters and change tangent types.**

Move Nearest Key Allows you to reposition keys by clicking and dragging.

Scene summary All keys of all objects.

Dope Sheet summary All keys of all selected objects.

Outliner Loaded objects are displayed in this window, where you can expand the hierarchy to view different attributes.

Objects

Attributes

Audio Current audio track.

Selected keys Keyframes can be selected by LM-clicking. Multiple keys can be selected by holding the Shift key or by LM-clicking and dragging.

Keys Individual keys show up as blocks.

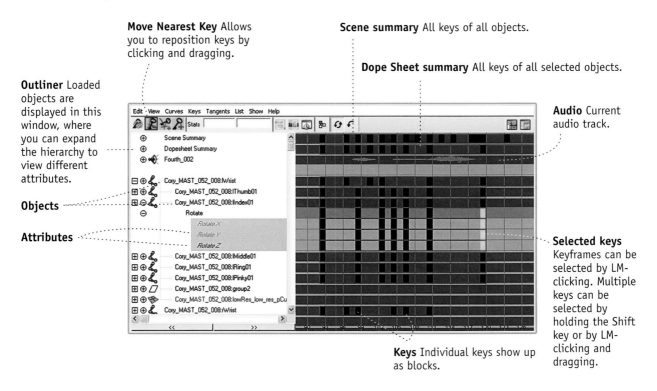

Types of Tangents

Tangents define how an object behaves before and after a specific keyframe. With tangents, you can sculpt the object's motion to get effects such as acceleration and deceleration as well as constant linear motion. Tangents can be applied in either the Graph Editor or the Dope Sheet. The Fixed tangent type (choose Tangents → Fixed) locks down tangents at their current position so that they are not recalculated if neighboring keyframes change.

TIP Maya's Pre and Post Infinity curves (choose View → Infinity in the Graph Editor) let you see how an object will move before and after the last key. You can cycle animation by choosing Curves → Pre Infinity and Curves → Post Infinity from the Graph Editor's Curves menu.

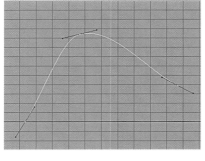

Spline: Creates a smooth transition along the curve, resulting in smooth, organic transitions from one key to the next.

Linear: This tangent offers no change in velocity and is good for objects moving at a constant rate of speed.

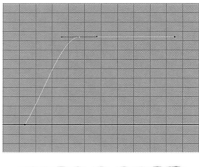

Clamped: A hybrid between spline and linear, it uses linear curves when values are nearly equal. These are used when an object needs to remain fixed for a period and then move organically.

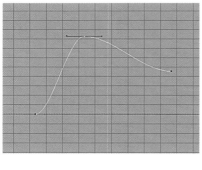

Flat: Offers linear motion through the majority of the curve, with slow-in and slow-out at either end.

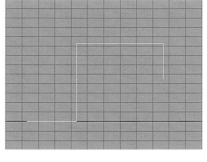

Stepped: Simply jumps from one key to the next. Useful for mechanical attributes that are either on or off, such as a switched light.

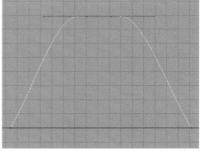

Plateau: Spline curves that ease-in to a flat tangent, and then ease-out back to a spline curve.

Tangent Weights

Adjusting the handles of the tangents by MM-clicking and dragging allows you to change the angle of the tangent. The size and weight of the tangent, however, does not change. To adjust the tangent's weight, select the curve and choose Curves → Weighted Tangents. You can then select the desired key and choose Keys → Free Tangent Weight. This gives you complete control over the size and angle of the tangent.

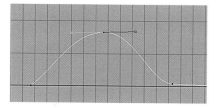

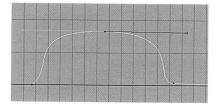

Graph Editor

The Graph Editor displays keyframes as curves. These curves not only display keys, but also the interpolation between keys, giving you complete control over the animation.

Move Nearest Key Allows you to reposition keys by clicking and dragging.

Tangent types These buttons quickly change the tangent type of the selected keys.

Tangent controls Tools to manipulate the tangents for animation curves.

Insert Keys Places new keys on an existing animation curve.

Add Keys Adds keys to an existing curve, maintaining the value of the attribute at the current frame.

Lattice Deform Keys Lets you draw a lattice deformer around groups of keys so that you can manipulate many keys at once.

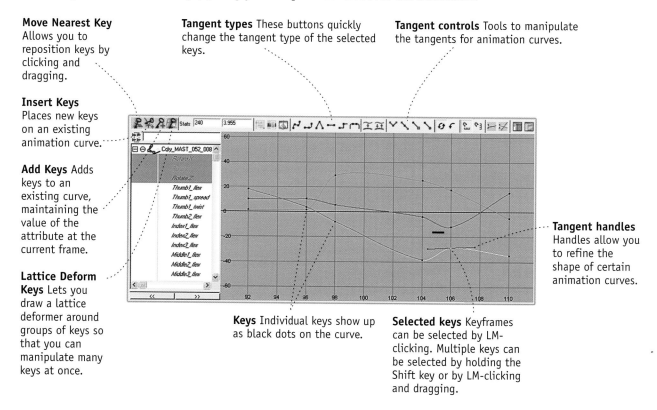

Tangent handles Handles allow you to refine the shape of certain animation curves.

Keys Individual keys show up as black dots on the curve.

Selected keys Keyframes can be selected by LM-clicking. Multiple keys can be selected by holding the Shift key or by LM-clicking and dragging.

Character Animation

Animating a character involves setting a lot of keys for a lot of different joints, IK handles, objects, and blend shapes. Maya has several tools that allow you to easily manage this wide range of attributes and keep your mind focused on the task at hand—bringing a character to life.

Character Sets

Character sets allow you to collect all the attributes associated with a character in one place so you can have broader control over your character. Setting keys on a character set will set keys for all the associated attributes, making it easy to animate the entire character a pose at a time.

To create a character set, choose Character → Create Character Set. This creates an empty character. To add attributes to the character set, select the desired attributes from the Channel box or the Attribute Editor and choose Character → Add To Character Set. You can also edit character sets in the Relationship Editor.

TIP You can create subcharacters to further define a character. You can create different subcharacters for different parts of the body. For example, you can set subcharacter keys for just the legs or the arms.

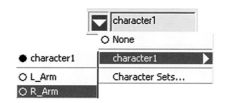

Characters are selected on the bottom-right corner of the screen. If subcharacters are defined, a second menu appears.

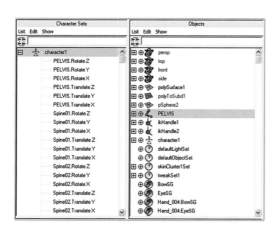

The Relationship Editor is used to edit character sets.

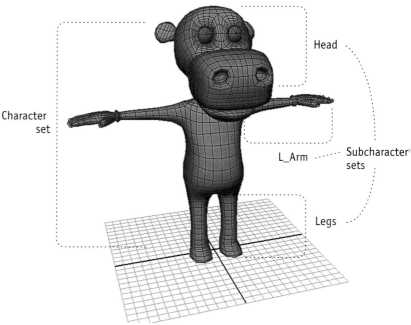

Character sets comprise the entire character and all its attributes; subcharacter sets segment the character into parts.

Animating with Character Sets

Character sets allow you to animate characters a pose at a time. Rather than worrying about each individual joint, you animate the entire character (or subcharacter). Setting a key for a character set is as simple as setting a key for any attribute within that character. When a character is active, keying one attribute in a character set sets a key for all the other attributes. These keys, however, can still be edited individually in the Dope Sheet or the Graph Editor.

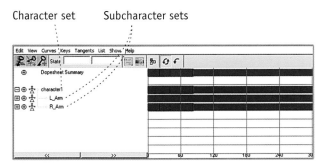

Character set   Subcharacter sets

You can edit keys for the entire character set just as you would for any other attribute. When selected, the character set shows up in the Outliner section of the Dope Sheet and Graph Editor.

Trax

Trax is Maya's nonlinear animation editor. Trax stores animation as clips, which can be dragged and dropped on the Trax Editor window, where they can be layered, trimmed, and edited to create whole new sequences. Trax allows you to edit motion above the keyframe level, giving broad control over animation and motion capture data.

Animation used in Trax must be part of a character set. If you create a clip for an object that is not already part of a character set, the Trax Editor automatically creates a new character for the clip.

File Allows you to import and export clips. Clips can also be dragged and dropped directly from the Visor window.

View Tools to change the way the tracks are viewed. Animation curves can be viewed using the Graph Editor, which can be launched from here.

Create Tools to create clips, poses, and character sets as well as effects such as blends and time warps.

Toolbar Shortcuts for the most frequently used menu items.

Edit Tools to edit the clips. In addition to Cut and Paste, tools to split and trim the selected clips.

Track controls Controls to lock, solo, and mute tracks.

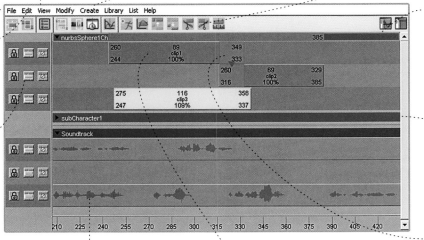

Character track Each character has a master track, which allows you to move and scale the entire sequence.

Subcharacter tracks If a character is divided into subcharacters, the subcharacter clips appear here.

Blend A blend between two clips.

Audio Multiple audio tracks can be used.

Clip Clips can contain animation, motion capture, or individual poses.

The Trax Editor window

Clips

A clip is simply a collection of animation curves for a particular character. Clips let you gather a character's keyframe or motion capture data into a single place so Trax can manipulate the character all at once.

Drag top corners to trim

275	116	358
	clip3	
-247	109%	337

Drag bottom corners to scale

Drag middle to move

When you create a clip, two kinds of clips are generated: a source clip and a regular clip. The source clip is added to the character's scene, and the regular clip is inserted under its character in the Trax Editor. The source clip is essentially the "master" copy, but the regular clip can be trimmed, stretched, and edited on the Timeline.

In addition to regular clips, Trax also allows you to create constraint and expression clips. These clips hold only constraint or expression data. A constraint clip, for example, can be used when a character picks up an object.

Poses

A pose is simply a clip that is only one frame long. Poses are used extensively in character animation. Many times a character will need to strike a strong pose, which can be created by a lead animator and then used by other members of the team. Trax can be used in between these poses to create animation.

Poses can also be used to create snapshots of parts of the animation. If you need a character to return to a specific pose, for example, you can take a snapshot of that pose and use it as a target in Trax. This method can also be used to take a snapshot of blend shape combinations for facial animation.

Animating with Trax

Creating animation using Trax requires a library of clips. Building the library may take a lot of time, but the initial investment pays off when new animation needs to be created. This work flow makes Trax ideally suited for longer projects, such as games or a television series, in which animation can be reused.

Clips can be stored and managed using the Visor window. You can edit clips at the key level by choosing View → Graph Anim Curves, which opens the Graph Editor.

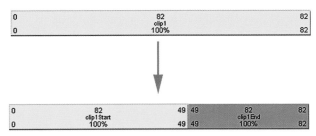

Splitting clips: To split a clip, select the clip, position the Time slider at the split point, and then choose Edit → Split from the Trax window.

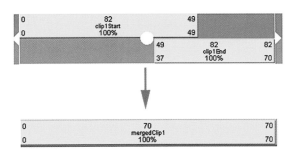

Merging clips: Clips can be merged by selecting the clips and then choosing Edit → Merge from the Trax menu.

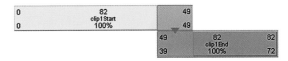

Blends: Blends allow for a seamless transition from one clip to another. Select the two clips and choose Create → Blend from the Trax menu.

Anim Clip Attributes

☑ Enable

Weight	1.000
Weight Style	From Start
Start Frame	125.000
Pre Cycle	0.000
Post Cycle	0.000
Scale	1.000
Hold	0.000
Source Start	125.000
Source End	324.000
☐ Time Warp Enable	
Time Warp	0.000

Clips can also be edited in the Attribute Editor. Here you can modify the start and end times, as well as add cycles or hold animation at the end of the clip.

TIP   With the Character Mapper window, you can transfer animation between characters. The window allows you to connect attributes of one character to another. This is particularly useful in motion capture or when reusing animation.

Walk Cycle

1 Open the file Ch09_Walk-Start.mb. This has a rigged character with a rig similar to the one created in the previous chapter.

2 Start the walk with the legs. Move the Time slider to frame 0. Select the IK handles at the ankles, and position the feet so they are apart with the right foot forward. Select and move the pelvis so it is halfway between the feet. Rotate the pelvis slightly so that the right hip is forward. Set keys for all IK handles (including the toes) and the pelvis.

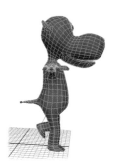

3 Move the Time slider to frame 6. Turn on Auto Key to make keyframing easier. Select the pelvis and move it up and forward so that it is above the right foot. Select the IK handle at the left foot, and move it forward and up so that it is off the ground at the point where it passes the right leg. Adjust the IK handle at the left toe to point the toe down.

4 Move the Time slider to frame 12, and create a mirror pose to that on frame 0, with the left foot forward and the pelvis rotated so the left hip is forward.

5 Repeat the same poses over frames 12–24, making the right foot pass the left at frame 18.

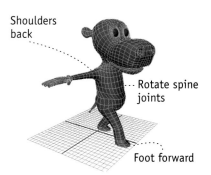

Shoulders back

Rotate spine joints

Foot forward

6 Now set some keys for the spine. As the pelvis rotates to the right, the spine and shoulders rotate to the left. Set keys at frames 0, 12, and 24 to create a balanced pose for the spine.

7 The arms are next. When the right foot is forward, the right hand is back, and vice versa.

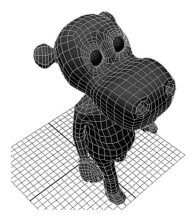

8 Finally, the head. Animate rotation on the head so that the character is facing forward.

Special Effects

M aya is used extensively as a special effects tool in the film, video, and game industries. Special effects can be created in a variety of ways, but many of the best special effects simulate reality. Maya has a number of tools for creating and animating objects that respond to real-world forces such as gravity, wind, and fields. Objects animated in this way can appear highly realistic and can seamlessly blend with real-world scenes.

Particles simulate the motion of large numbers of objects and are terrific for all sorts of fire, water, and atmospheric effects. Rigid Body dynamics allow objects to animate and collide with each other using forces, and Soft Body dynamics allow physical forces to affect the actual shape of an object.

Particle Effects

Particle systems are used to simulate all sorts of natural phenomena, from smoke and fire to rain, sparks, and any other effect that requires animating a large number of objects. In Maya, you animate particles using dynamics, which simulate real-world forces such as wind and gravity. To create a particle system, you need to set up an emitter to generate the particles and then define what the particles will look like.

Emitters

Particles originate in emitters. An emitter can control the type of particle as well as the particle's number, speed, direction, and rate of creation. You control these attributes either through the emitter's Attributes panel or by using the Show Manipulators option when the emitter is selected.

Rate The rate at which particles are emitted per frame.

Cycle You can set particles to cycle for game applications.

Min/Max Distance You can set particles to be created away from the emitter by increasing the minimum distance. Maximum distance is the farthest a particle can exist from the emitter.

Direction For a directional emitter, the direction the particles are emitted.

Emitter Type The type of emitter: Directional, Omni, Surface, Curve, or Volume.

Spread For a directional emitter, the spread of the particles.

Speed The speed of the particles, which can also be randomized to get a more natural effect.

Spread 0.25

The Show Manipulator tool can be used to interactively adjust an emitter's attributes, such as spread, emission rate, speed, distance, and direction.

Types of Emitters

Maya has several types of emitters. Emitters such as Directional, Volume, and Omni (choose Particles → Create Emitter) emit particles from a point or volume in space; Surface and Curve emitters (choose Particles → Emit From Object) emit particles from an object.

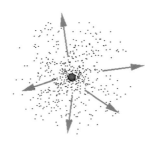

Directional: Much like a nozzle or a spotlight, the Directional emitter allows you to aim particles in a general direction and control the angle of spread.

Omni: Much like an omni light, the Omni emitter sends particles in all directions.

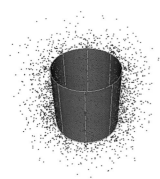

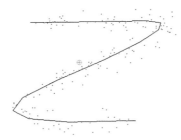

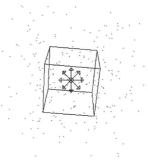

Surface: Any NURBS or polygonal surface can emit particles.

Curve: A NURBS curve can also emit particles.

Volume: Creates particles within a primitive volume, such as a cube, sphere, or cylinder.

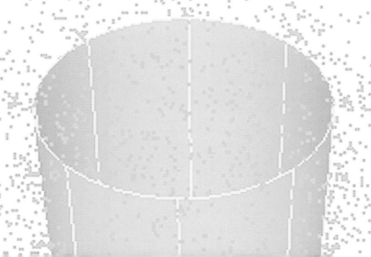

Particle Types

Particles in Maya can appear in a variety of ways. The type of particle you choose depends on the type of effect you want.

Points displays particles as points.

MultiPoint displays each particle as multiple points, which make the particles appear denser. This is good for dust, clouds, or gas.

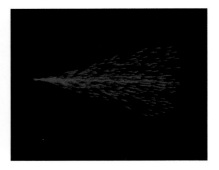

Streak displays particles with an elongated tail, which works well with meteors or fireworks.

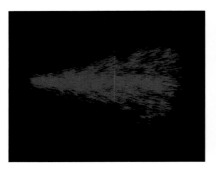

MultiStreak is a combination of Streak and MultiPoint and displays multiple points with tails for each moving particle.

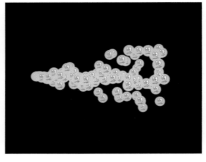

Sprites use a texture image or image sequence for each particle. You can use this to simulate effects such as smoke and clouds as well as other effects.

Sphere displays particles as opaque spheres.

Blobby Surface calculates particles as metaballs (spheres that blend together to form surfaces). It is perfect for liquid effects.

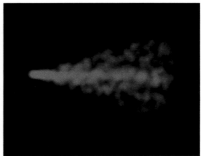

Cloud displays particles as blurred or cloudy metaballs. These are perfect for smoke and fire effects.

Particle Lifespans

Many types of effects require that the particles change over the course of their lifetimes. A red fire particle, for example, might change into a gray particle as it ages to simulate fire turning into smoke. Some effects can require a particle's opacity to change as it gets older. Particles can also increase or decrease in size.

When created, particles are given a set of creation rules. As they move through time, the particles are controlled by a set of runtime rules that determine how the particle will look, move, and react. These rules are set in the Per Particle (Array) Attributes rollout in the ParticleShape tab in the particle system's Attributes panel.

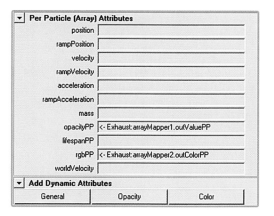

Per Particle attributes determine how a particle behaves over the course of its lifetime. Some common attributes are provided in the default rollout, but more can be added using the General, Opacity, and Color buttons.

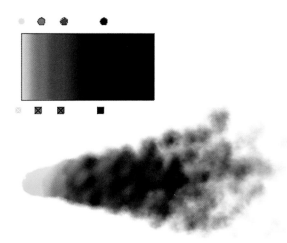
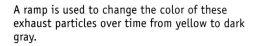

A ramp is used to change the color of these exhaust particles over time from yellow to dark gray.

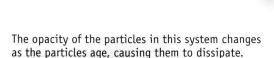

The opacity of the particles in this system changes as the particles age, causing them to dissipate.

Particle Collisions

Particles can collide with other objects in the scene, allowing for realistic interactions and effects. Any object can become a collision object. Simply select the particle system, select the object, and choose Particles → Make Collide. This will cause the particles to bounce off the selected object. A resilience attribute can be adjusted to make the particles lose energy as they strike the object.

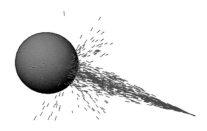

Particles can collide with objects in the scene for realistic effects.

Particle collision events (choose Particles → Particle Collision Events Editor) can make particles split or emit new particles when they collide with another object.

Affecting Particles with Fields

The motion of particles can be affected by fields. Fields can create such effects as gravity, wind, vortex, and turbulence. To connect a particle system to a field, select the particle system, select the field, and then choose Fields → Affect Selected Object(s). Another method is to select the particle system and then choose the desired field's icon from the Dynamics shelf.

A gravity field pulls objects in a specific direction, usually toward the ground.

A vortex field creates a swirling effect.

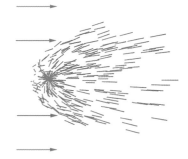

An air field acts much like the wind, blowing particles in a specific direction.

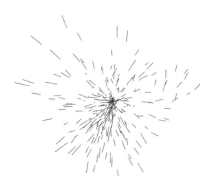

Turbulence fields add random turbulence to a particle system.

Rigid Body Dynamics

Rigid Body dynamics animates objects automatically to simulate the effect of real-world forces and collisions. This method creates highly realistic-looking animation and is good for simulating natural motion. It's also useful for those situations in which a large number of objects need to be animated, such as the debris of an explosion.

Active rigid bodies Objects that are affected by forces and are automatically animated during the simulation.

Fields Forces such as gravity, wind, and turbulence that affect rigid bodies.

Passive rigid bodies Objects that are not automatically animated but are nonetheless part of the simulation and act as collision objects.

A rigid body simulation has several components.

Mass Just as in nature, the more mass an object has, the more force it will take to move it.

Center Of Mass Adjusts the center of the object. A low center of mass makes an object more stable; a high center of mass makes an object top-heavy and prone to tipping.

Bounciness Determines how much energy an object loses when it collides. Values below 1 mean the object loses energy; above 1 adds energy.

Damping A force that acts to slow the object; similar to drag.

Friction Determines how much an object will resist motion when in contact with another object. Static friction is how sticky the object is while still; dynamic friction affects objects after they begin to move.

Rigid Body Attributes

☑ Active
☐ Particle Collision
☐ Allow Disconnection

Mass	1.000		
Center Of Mass	0.021	0.000	0.000
☐ Lock Center Of Mass			
Static Friction	0.200		
Dynamic Friction	0.200		
Bounciness	0.600		
Damping	0.000		
Impulse	0.000	0.000	0.000
Impulse Position	0.000	0.000	0.000
Spin Impulse	0.000	0.000	0.000

Impulse A constant force that is applied to an object at every frame. This can be a linear force or a rotational one (spin).

Initial Settings

Initial Spin	0.000	0.000	0.000
Initial Position	1.053	1.011	5.035
Initial Orientation	-55.875	0.000	0.000
Initial Velocity	0.000	0.000	0.000

A way to get things moving in a scene is to give objects an initial setting such as an initial velocity or spin.

Setting Up Rigid Body Simulations

A rigid body simulation usually requires both active and passive bodies as well as fields and some initial conditions, such as the mass of the objects, friction, and the object's initial velocities. Once you set up the initial parameters, you can run the simulation and bake the results into animation curves.

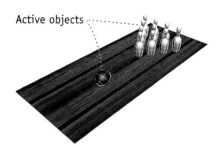

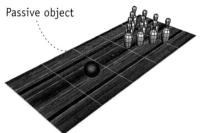

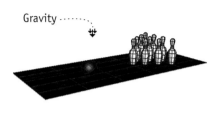

Create active bodies: In this simulation, the bowling ball and the pins will affect each other and thus will be active bodies. Select the objects and choose Soft/Rigid Bodies → Create Active Rigid Body.

Create passive bodies: The floor is a passive body and will remain rigid. Select the object and choose Soft/Rigid Bodies → Create Passive Rigid Body.

Add fields: To make sure the pins fall down, add gravity by choosing Fields → Gravity. The active objects are then selected along with the gravity field and connected when you choose Fields → Affect Selected Object(s).

Set initial conditions: The mass of the ball and pins are configured along with the initial velocity for the ball.

Run simulation: Clicking the Play button on the Timeline will calculate the simulation. You can then Bake this into animation curves by choosing Edit → Keys → Bake Simulation.

Dynamic Constraints

Many times, objects are connected together and need to affect the motion of other objects. Dynamic constraints connect the motion of one object to another. There are several types of dynamic constraints.

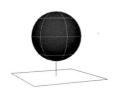

Nail: Connects a rigid body to a specific point in space.

Pin: Connects two rigid bodies at a point.

Hinge: Constrains a rigid body's motion to a specific axis, much like the hinge of a door.

Spring: Connects two bodies using an elasticlike connection.

Barrier: Creates a hard barrier defined by a plane. Bodies cannot pass this plane.

Soft Body Dynamics

Soft bodies use dynamics to affect the shape of an object. Soft bodies are great for secondary motion such as a waving flag, a jiggling belly, or a dog's floppy ears. Soft bodies work by adding a particle to each control point or vertex of an object. Fields or the objects can then affect these particles to deform the object's shape.

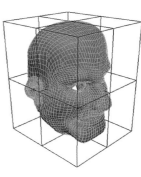

Deforming the lattice using a soft body saves calculation time and achieves nearly the same result as deforming the complex mesh.

Soft bodies can be created from curves, NURBS surfaces, or polygonal geometry. Lattices, wire deformers, motion paths, and wrap deformers can also use soft bodies as a way to deform their shape. Turning a deformer into a soft body can save calculation time on complex meshes.

Soft bodies were used to deform this character's belly to make it jiggle as he walks.

Creating Soft Bodies

Soft bodies are created by selecting the target object and choosing Soft/Rigid Bodies →
Create Soft Body. Creating a soft body creates a particle system that contains a particle for
every vertex, CV, lattice point, or other control point in the object. These particles then
drive the deformation of the object itself by animating the object's control points.

The flag is turned into a soft
body.

This creates a particle system with one particle per
surface CV.

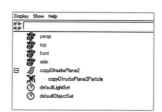

In the Outliner, these
particles are contained in
a separate object with its
own attributes.

Because the soft body
objects are particles, they
can be animated using the
same dynamics tools used
for particle systems, such as
gravity fields, air fields, and
turbulence.

Goals

Goals are target shapes for the soft body. Think of a goal as a "rest position" for
the particles, as they will always try to go back to this shape, depending on the
goal weights. The goal is typically a copy of the deformed object.

In the Attributes panel for the soft
body's particles, you can set goal
weights for all the particles.

Individual weights can be edited in the Component Editor.

The Paint Soft Body Weights
tool sets goal weights by
painting on the soft body
surface with an Artisan
brush. The brush can be set
to add, subtract, or smooth
the weighting map. Weights
display as a range of
grayscale values, with a
weight of 1 displaying as
white and 0 as black.

Creating Rocket Exhaust

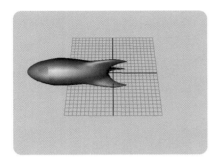

1 From the companion CD, open the file Ch10_RocketStart.mb. We will add an exhaust plume to this rocket using particles. First create an emitter for the particles: choose Particles → Create Emitter.

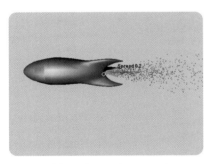

2 Position the emitter at the base of the rocket. In the emitter's Attributes panel, set Emitter Type to Directional, Rate to 250, Spread to 0.2, and Speed to 5.0. If you want, you can adjust these using the manipulator. Scrub the Time slider to see the particles.

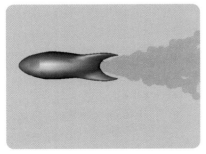

3 Now that we have particles, we need to make them look like smoke. Click the ParticleShape1 tab

in the Attributes panel. This panel controls the look of the particles. First, in the Render Attributes tab, set Particle Render Type to Cloud. Scrub the Time slider, and you'll see that the particles are now circular blobs.

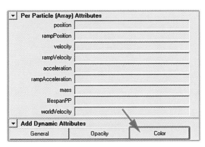

4 We need to add some color to the blobs. Go to the Per Particle (Array) Attributes → Add Dynamic Attributes rollout and click the Color button to open a dialog box.

5 We want the color to affect each particle individually, so select Add Per Particle Attribute and click Add Attribute.

```
Edit Ramp
Edit Array Mapper
Create rgbUPP -> arrayMapper1.uCoordPP
Break Connection
Delete Array Mapper
```

6 This adds an Attribute slot called rgbPP to the Per Particle Attributes rollout. Right-click this slot, and choose Create Ramp. This will add a value into the rgbPP slot. Right-click the slot again and choose Edit Ramp.

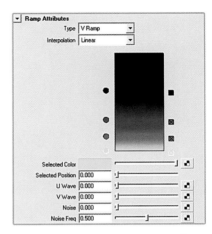

7 We can now create a ramp for the color of the exhaust over the lifetime of a particle. The bottom of the ramp is the color of the particle when the particle is created; the top color is its color when it expires. Create yellow at the start of the ramp, fading to red, and then dark gray at the end.

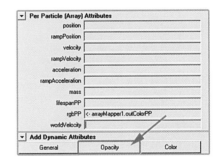

8 We also need to fade the particles to transparent to simulate dissipating smoke. This is done with opacity. Just like with the color, we need to add an opacity slot and create a ramp. Click the Opacity button on the Add Dynamic Attributes rollout, choose Add Per Particle Attribute, click Add Attribute from the dialog box that pops up, right-click the new slot to create a ramp, and then right-click again and choose Edit Ramp.

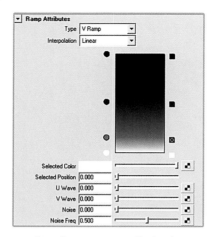

9 Opacity ramps are limited to grayscale, so create a ramp that starts white and fades to black.

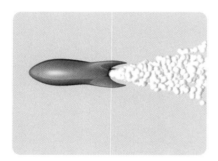

10 If you do a quick render, you'll see that the color is not showing up. This is because we still have to modify the particle system's shader.

11 Select the particles coming from the emitter. In the particle system's Attributes panel, locate the Lambert tab. Click the box

to the right of the Color attribute to open the Create Render Node window. Choose Utilities → Particle Utilities, and select Particle Sampler. This tells the shader to use the color ramp we just created. Repeat this procedure for the transparency channel.

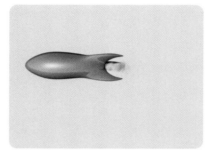

12 Scrub the Time slider to see the results. A test render shows the color is correct, but the particles are expiring too soon.

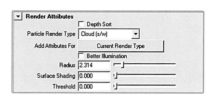

13 To fix this, go back to the ParticleShape1 tab in the Attributes panel and locate the Lifespan Attributes rollout. Set Lifespan Mode to Constant and increase Lifespan to 4.5.

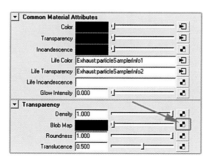

14 Locate the ParticleCloud1 tab in the Attributes panel. Click the box to the right of the Blob Map attribute to open the Create Render Node window. Choose a cloud texture. While in the ParticleCloud1 tab, adjust Diffuse Coeff to 0.9.

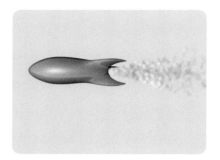

15 A scrub and a quick render shows that we're almost there. The particles are still a little small.

16 Move back to the Particle-Shape1 tab and locate the Render Attributes rollout. Click the Current Render Type button to reveal the attributes for this type of particle. Adjust the particle size to approximately 2.1. You can also play with the Threshold attribute to make the clouds blob together more.

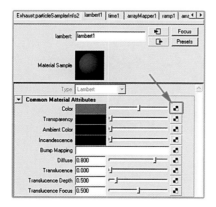

17 That should be it. Do a final render and go back to tweak any colors or other attributes to your liking.

MEL Script

```
switch ($nameOfSelectedHat)
{
  case "brownHat":
    print ("The brown hat is selected.");
    break;
  case "blueHat":
    print ("The blue hat is selected.");
    break;
  case "greenHat":
    print ("The green hat is selected.");
    break;
  case "redHat":
    print ("The red hat is selected.");
    break;
  default:
    print ("The hat name is unknown.");
    break;
}
```

Results:
The green hat is selected.

S cripting is a topic often daunting to artists who prefer a more-visual, user-friendly approach to content creation. Fortunately for artists, Maya's Maya Embedded Language (MEL) script is a high-level language that is tightly integrated within the rest of the program. In fact, just about everything in Maya is driven by MEL—even its interface!

With a little bit of practice, artists can realize that integrating MEL into their work flow is crucial for optimizing any part of the production pipeline. This chapter takes a visual approach to explaining the basics of MEL scripting.

What Is Scripting?

A script, as opposed to a program, is a series of commands that are interpreted line by line, rather than being compiled. A scripting language always exists within a program (in this case, Maya), and just about any runtime operation can be controlled by using a bit of MEL. Think of an executing MEL script as reading a book—you begin reading left to right, top to bottom. If you come across something that makes no sense, you assume there is an error. Similarly if the syntax of a line of script is incorrect, the script cannot continue and will notify you that an error occurred.

So what specifically could you do with MEL? If you are a modeler, you could use it to generate hundreds of randomly sized and shaped rocks. If you are an animator, you could create a custom user interface (UI) to easily keyframe common rig controls. You can use MEL script to save hours of arduous work pretty much anywhere in the production pipeline.

Using the Script Editor

The Script Editor allows you to input lines of MEL script in order to be executed or saved for later use. To open the editor, choose Window → General Editors → Script Editor.

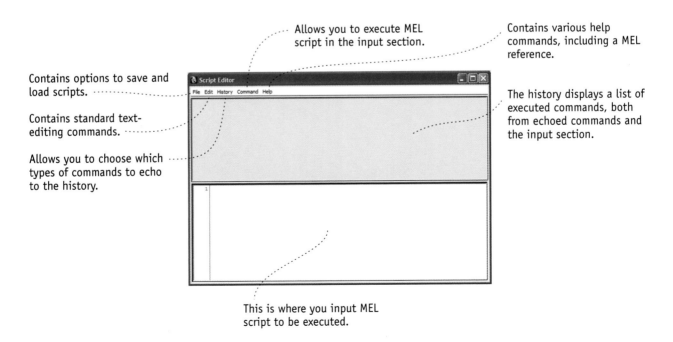

Allows you to execute MEL script in the input section.

Contains various help commands, including a MEL reference.

Contains options to save and load scripts.

Contains standard text-editing commands.

Allows you to choose which types of commands to echo to the history.

The history displays a list of executed commands, both from echoed commands and the input section.

This is where you input MEL script to be executed.

Almost every basic action in Maya is driven by a single or set of underlying MEL commands. The Script Editor allows you to peek at these commands so that you can learn and quickly create complex script-driven actions. Turn on command echoing by choosing History → Echo All Commands in the Script Editor. When choosing an action from a menu, such as Create → Polygon Primitives → Sphere, the history section of the Script Editor will echo the command in script syntax. With basically no programming knowledge, you can copy and paste together intricate scripts.

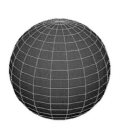
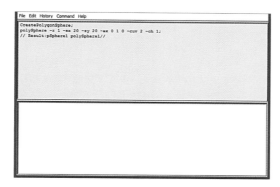

By looking at the Script Editor's history after creating a polygon sphere through the Create menu, you can discover the specific MEL command for creating a polygon sphere: polySphere.

To execute code in the input pane of the Script Editor, highlight the code with the mouse and choose Command → Execute, or press Ctrl+Enter/⌘+Return.

Source Script

Sourcing allows you to execute the contents of a saved MEL script. To source a script, choose File → Source Script in the Script Editor. When sourcing, local procedures are not initialized or executed. If the script file changes after you source it, you will need to source it again for Maya to notice the changes.

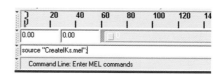

Shelves

Shelves are very useful for customizing your interface with quick, easy-access buttons for your favorite commands. You can add MEL scripts or portions of scripts to a shelf by selecting the code and choosing File → Save Script To Shelf. Alternatively, you can MMB-drag a selected script to a shelf.

Getting Help with MEL

MEL, as with any other major scripting or programming language, has thousands of commands, flags, and syntax rules. No artist is expected to know every command or syntax. Even the most seasoned technical artists use help documentation and references when scripting. Maya provides several ways for you to get help and understand any MEL command.

Using the Help Function

Maya's help function allows you to get a complete reference on how to use any function or command. In the input section of the Script Editor, type **help** followed by the name of the function you wish to learn more about. For instance, if the following is entered into the input pane:

```
help polySphere;
```

then the result in the history pane is as follows:

```
help polySphere;
// Result:

Synopsis: polySphere [flags] [String...]
Flags:
   -e -edit
   -q -query
  -ax -axis                 Length Length Length
 -cch -caching              on|off
  -ch -constructionHistory  on|off
 -cuv -createUVs            Int
   -n -name                 String
 -nds -nodeState            Int
   -o -object               on|off
   -r -radius               Length
  -sa -subdivisionsAxis     Int
  -sh -subdivisionsHeight   Int
  -sx -subdivisionsX        Int
  -sy -subdivisionsY        Int
  -tx -texture              Int

    //
```

These flags represent attributes that can be set when you call the polySphere command. Each of the flags has a default value in the event they are not specified. Flags can be listed in any order, and usually have shorthand and longhand notation. The list on the right hand refers to the data type for the flag. Suppose you want to create a polygon sphere with a radius of 5 units and named MyCoolSphere. You could execute the following command:

```
polySphere -radius 5 -name MyCoolSphere
```

Alternatively, you can use shorthand notation to abbreviate the radius and name flags:

```
polySphere -r 5 -n MyCoolSphere
```

The help function has several useful flags of its own, particularly the -doc flag. This flag will open your default web browser to Maya's web-based MEL reference, which typically has more detail and even examples about the function you need help with. To view the reference docs on the polySphere command, execute the following line:

```
help -doc polySphere
```

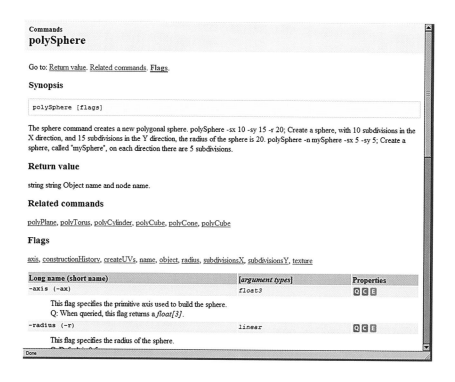

Debugging MEL

Because even the most seasoned programmer makes syntax mistakes, Maya supports warning and error checking. Warnings are flagged to the user in Command Feedback and Script Editor, but do not interrupt the script's execution. Errors, however, do stop the script and attempt to explain what the problem may be.

Warnings contain helpful solutions to potentially wrong scripting.

Errors are fatal to a script and will terminate on the offending line. Maya indicates possible reasons for the error.

Commenting

Commenting allows the script to contain documentation right along with the code. In MEL, line comments are identified by two forward slashes (//), and they can be inserted anywhere in code. To comment a block of text that spans multiple lines, use the forward slash and asterisk (/*) to begin the comment, and asterisk and forward slash (*/) to end the comment. Anything following the forward slashes will be ignored when the script executes. Commenting is good practice that helps readability for both yourself and others who may view your code.

```
/* This script generates a random
number of cubes */

// choose a random number (max 100)
int $NumberOfCubes = rand(100);

// loop to create the cubes
while ($NumberOfCubes > 0)
{
        // create a poly cube
        polyCube;

        // decrement counter
        $NumberOfCubes--;
}
```

Setting Attributes

An attribute is an editable property that describes how an object looks or behaves. There are many times when you will need to change certain attributes of an object in your scripts. To set an attribute for a specific object, use the following function:

```
setAttr [flags] objectName.attributeName value;
```

When creating a geometric primitive, such as a sphere, there are really two nodes at work: the shape node and the transform node. The shape node contains inputs that hold attributes specific to the object's calculated shape, such as the radius of a sphere or the number of subdivisions in a cube. The transform node handles basic transform attributes, such as translation, rotation, and scale. Be sure to edit attributes on the correct node, or Maya will flag a script error message.

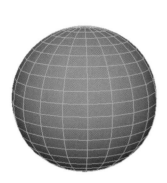

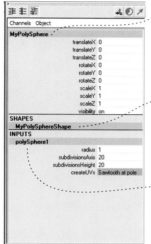

The transform node handles all basic transform attributes including translation, rotation, scale, and visibility.

The shape node is made up of inputs that determine the object's shape.

Inputs hold attributes that modify the shape node of an object.

```
polySphere -name MyPolySphere;
```

A polygon sphere named MyPolySphere with default attributes.

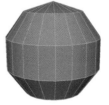

```
setAttr polySphere1.subdivisionsHeight 5;
```

The number of subdivisions along the height of the sphere changed from the default 20 to 5.

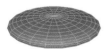

```
setAttr MyPolySphere.scaleY 0.2;
```

The scaleY attribute changed from the default 1.0 to 0.2.

```
setAttr MyPolySphere.rz 90;
```

The rotateZ attribute changed from default 0 to 90. This example uses shorthand notation for the rotateZ attribute.

Using Variables

Values can be assigned to variables, a named memory location that stores data that can be used in a variety of ways. There are a few basic rules when using variables with MEL:

Basic Rules of MEL Variables

Variable names must begin with a dollar sign ($).

The variable name can include only letters, numbers, and underscores.

The first character after the dollar sign cannot be a number.

Variables must be declared before they can be used.

Declaring variables means that you tell Maya the name of the variable you intend to use and what type of data it is. MEL supports the following data types:

1, 7, 0, 36, 1003, ...

Int: An integer representing whole numbers

```
int $MyVariable = 5;
```

"Maya", "Hi there", "This is a string"

String: A set of characters to store a word or sentence

```
string $MyVariable = "MEL script is fun!";
```

3.14159, 2.8, 0.05

Float: A floating-point number representing a real number (with a decimal)

```
float $MyVariable = 5.32;
```

(5.2, 3.6, 40), (255, 20, 255)

Vector: Holds three numbers that typically represent 3D coordinates (X, Y, Z) and color (red, green, blue)

```
vector $MyVariable = <<2, 3.2, 4>>;
```

[1, 2, 3, 4, 5], [3.09, 2.334, 8], ["this", "that"]

Array: Holds lists of integers, floats, strings, or vectors, used for storing various amounts of similar data

```
int $MyVariable[4] = {7, 11, 13, 17};
float $MyVariable[4] = {7.1, 11.2, 13.0, 17.992};
string $MyVariable[4] = {"first", "second", "third", "fourth"};
```

$$\begin{bmatrix} 4.3, 2.1, 4.5, 8.2 \\ 5.3, 23.1, 0.1, 2.1 \end{bmatrix}$$

Matrix: A two-dimensional table of floating-point numbers

```
matrix $MyVariable[2][4] = <<4.3, 2.1, 4.5, 8.2;
                            5.3, 23.1, 0.1, 2.1>>
```

Accessing Elements

Vectors, arrays, and matrices are all known as data structures. They contain and encapsulate multiple numbers or strings. You can read and write to the specific values within the data structure; however, vectors, arrays, and matrices each have their own ways of doing this.

Vectors

Because vectors are typically used to represent coordinates, their elements are referenced by .x, .y, and .z accessors:

```
vector $MyVector = <<2.4, 4.5, 6.7>>;
print($MyVector.x); // prints out 2.4
print($MyVector.y); // prints out 4.5
print($MyVector.z); // prints out 6.7
```

   You cannot change the value for one specific element of the vector. If you want to change the contents of an element, you must supply the entire new vector, even if the other elements are unchanged:

```
vector $MyVector = <<2.4, 4.5, 6.7>>;
$MyVector = <<$MyVector.x, 9.1, $MyVector.z>>;
```

Arrays

Specific elements of an array can be accessed by specifying the array name along with an index value in square brackets. The index is an integer that refers to the spot within the array where a particular piece of data resides. Note that the index of the first element is always 0:

```
float $MyArray[3] = {10, 20, 30};
print($MyArray[0]); // prints out 10
print($MyArray[1]); // prints out 20
print($MyArray[2]); // prints out 30
```

   You can change the contents of an indexed array slot by specifying a new value for the slot. Arrays are dynamic, meaning their length can change at any time by adding or removing elements. You can add elements by specifying an index; if the index exceeds the current size of the array, the array grows to the new index size:

```
float $MyArray[3] = {10, 20, 30};
$MyArray[0] = 40; // array is now {40, 20, 30}
$MyArray[3] = 50; // array is now {40, 20, 30, 50}
$MyArray[5] = 60; // array is now {40, 20, 30, 50, 0, 60}
```

[0] [1] [2] [3] [4]

Matrices

Think of a matrix as a two-dimensional array, in that instead of one number serving as an index, there are now two. An index in a matrix is specified by first the row and then the column:

```
matrix $MyMatrix[3][5] = <<1.1, 2.3, 3.6, 4.8, 5.2;
                           6.9, 5.3, 0.2, 9.1, 3.2;
                           5.7, 9.6, 4.2, 5.1, 7.9>>
```

You can change the contents of a matrix slot as with an array; however, the size of matrices is not dynamic. After a matrix has been declared, the number of rows and columns cannot change. Like arrays, index values always begin at 0:

```
matrix $MyMatrix[3][5] = <<1.1, 2.3, 3.6, 4.8, 5.2;
                           6.9, 5.3, 0.2, 9.1, 3.2;
                           5.7, 9.6, 4.2, 5.1, 7.9>>
$MyMatrix[0][0] = 3.3; // [0][0] changed from 1.1 to 3.3
$MyMatrix[1][3] = 7.5; // [1][3] changed from 9.1 to 7.5
$MyMatrix[2][4] = 1.0; // [2][4] changed from 7.9 to 1.0
```

Looping

Often during scripts, you will need something to happen a specified number of times. One major advantage to scripting is that it can handle a lot of the mundane, repetitive work such as creating 100 objects so that each has a slightly different color, or iterating through all your selections and performing actions. This kind of iteration is called looping, and there are several ways to do it in MEL, including the standard for loop, for-in loop, while loop, and do-while loop.

For Loop

The standard for loop has the following syntax:

```
for (initial_value; test_value; increment)
```

> **TIP** The plus-plus (++) symbol after a variable means that the variable increments its value by one. Minus-minus (−−) decrements the value by one.

The following code demonstrates an example of a for loop:

```
// variable used for incrementing through the for loop
int $i;
// do the following code 10 times
for ($i = 1; $i <= 10; $i++)
{
  // create a new cylinder
  polyCylinder;
  // rotate the cylinder 15 degrees times $i about X
  rotate -r (15 * $i) 0 0;
  // move the cylinder 3 units times $i down Z
  move -r 0 0 (3 * $i);
}
```

This script demonstrates creating 10 cylinders, rotating each 15 degrees more than the previous cylinder, and moving each 3 units to the right.

Listing Objects

A common scripting need is listing object names in the scene, whether it be all the user-selected objects, all the objects of a specific type, or just all the objects in the scene. The following are some examples of a few frequently used commands:

Command	Action
ls;	Lists all the objects in the scene
ls -selection	Lists all the selected objects
ls "LeftArm"	Lists the object named LeftArm
ls "*Boards"	Lists all the objects ending with Boards
ls -geometry	Lists all the geometry object types

> **TIP** Surrounding a command with backquotes (` `) causes immediate evaluation of the command. You can assign the results of the command to a variable.

The following code demonstrates an example of listing objects:

```
// declare a string to iterate through the loop
string $currentObject;
// assign the current selection to a string array
string $sel[] = `ls -sl`;
// loop over every item in the selection
for ($currentObject in $sel)
{
    print ($currentObject+ "\n");
}
Results:
BackBoards
SeatBoards
RightArm
LeftArm
```

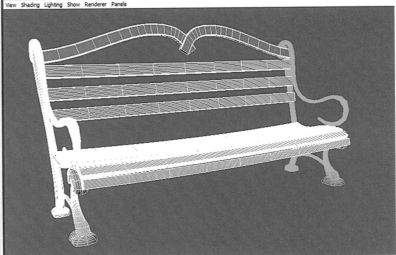

Branching

Often while scripting, you will need to ask a question such as, "Is this object at the origin?" and then do something if it is true or do something else if it is false. Branching handles this kind of logic with if...else and switch statements.

if...else Statements

Using if statements is the most common way to create conditional logic in MEL. Although not required, an else statement after an if statement offers an alternative if the condition is false. An if...else statement has the following syntax:

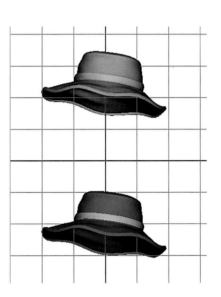

```
if (test)
{
    Commands;
}
else
{
    Commands;
}
```

The following code demonstrates an example of an if statement:

```
if (getAttr("brownHat.translateY") > getAttr("redHat.translateY"))
{
  print("The brown hat is above the red hat.");
}
else if (getAttr("brownHat.translateY") < getAttr("redHat.translateY"))
{
  print ("The brown hat is below the red hat.");
}
else
{
  print ("The brown and red hats are at the same level.");
}

Results:
The brown hat is above the red hat.
```

switch Statements

A switch statement branches by comparing a control to cases. If the control equals the case value, then the commands within the case are executed. In the event that a control fails all the cases, a default case will execute. Switches have the following syntax:

```
switch (control)
{
  case value1:
    commands;
    break;
  case value2:
    commands;
    break;
  ...
  default:
    commands;
    break;
}
```

The following code demonstrates an example of a switch statement:

```
switch ($nameOfSelectedHat)
{
  case "brownHat":
    print ("The brown hat is selected.");
    break;
  case "blueHat":
    print ("The blue hat is selected.");
    break;
  case "greenHat":
    print ("The green hat is selected.");
    break;
  case "redHat":
    print ("The red hat is selected.");
    break;
  default:
    print ("The hat name is unknown.");
    break;
}
```

```
Results:
The green hat is selected.
```

GUI Windows

Creating windows with visual controls and feedback is much more user-friendly than running scripts in the Command line or Script Editor. There are two necessary components to every Maya GUI: a `window` command and a `showWindow` command.

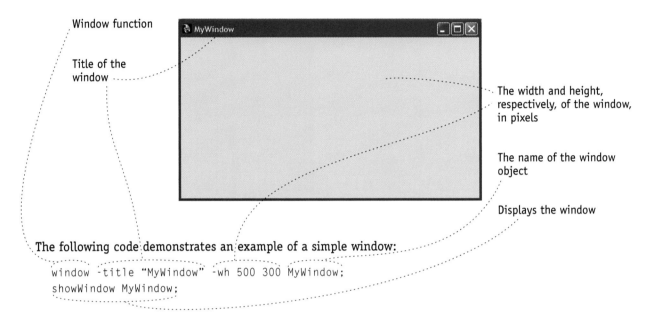

Window function

Title of the window

The width and height, respectively, of the window, in pixels

The name of the window object

Displays the window

The following code demonstrates an example of a simple window:

```
window -title "MyWindow" -wh 500 300 MyWindow;
showWindow MyWindow;
```

Layouts

Layouts control the general formatting of other UI elements. There are many options for arranging the controls and data in your window. Typically, the layout type is declared in the line after the window declaration. Some layout types, such as pane, tab, and scroll, allow you to embed different layout types within a parent layout.

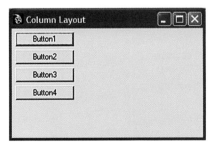

Column Layout: Arranges UI elements into columns

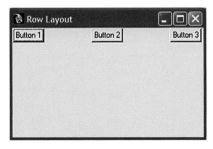

Row Layout: Arranges UI elements into rows

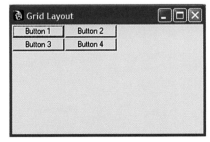

Grid Layout: Arranges UI elements into grids, left to right, top to bottom

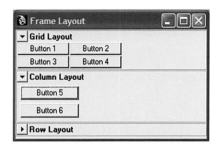

Frame Layout: Groups UI elements into frames that can contain their own layout types

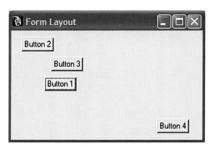

Form Layout: A free-form layout that uses pixel values to determine the placement of UI elements

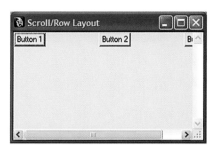

Scroll/Row Layout: When placed before another layout, allows for horizontal and vertical scroll bars

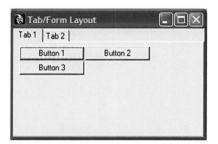

Tab/Form Layout: Arranges UI elements inside tabs that can contain their own layout types

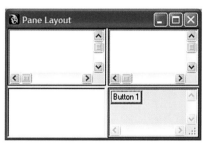

Pane Layout: Arranges UI elements inside panes that can contain their own layout types

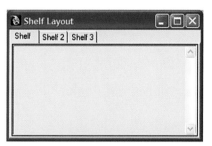

Shelf Layout: Arranges UI elements inside shelves that can contain their own layout types

Controls

Maya offers a wide variety of common controls to allow for user interaction. Controls are the medium by which users input commands into a GUI window and can be linked to commands and scripts. Some controls are grouped with other basic controls, such as a slider with a text box linked to the slider's value, to help streamline common control usage. The following are some primary controls; type help -doc followed by the control's command to see a list of all the flags and creation options.

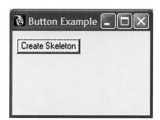

```
button -label "Create Skeleton";
```

Button: Displays a label text and executes a command when selected by the user.

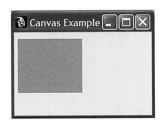

```
canvas -rgbValue  1 0.5 0 -width 150 -height 75;
```

Canvas: Displays a color swatch. It usually is paired with an action to open a color chooser.

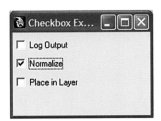

```
checkBox -label "Log Output" -align left;
```

Checkbox: Has an on/off toggle field and a text label. It is best used for true/false settings.

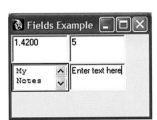

```
floatField -minValue -10 -maxValue 10 -value 1.42;
intField -minValue -10 -maxValue 10 -value 5;
scrollField -wordWrap true -text "My Notes";
textField;
```

Field: Allows the user to type input in the window. The type of field controls the kind of data that can be entered. The four most common fields are float, integer, scroll, and text.

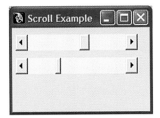

```
floatScrollBar -min -5.5 -max 43.5 -value 20.3 -step 1 -largeStep 5;
intScrollBar -min 0 -max 50 -value 15 -step 1 -largeStep 10;
```

Scrollbar: Users can scroll a bar to specify a value within the scrollbar's range. The step flag refers to how much the bar moves when the arrows are selected, and the large step flag determines how much the bar jumps when the control background is selected. A float scrollbar can handle floating-point numbers, whereas an int scrollbar can handle only integer values.

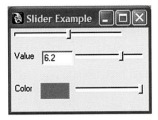

```
floatSlider -min -100 -max 100 -value 0 -step 1;
floatSliderGrp -label "Value" -field true
     -minValue -10.0 -maxValue 10.0
     -fieldMinValue -100.0 -fieldMaxValue 100.0
     -value 0;
colorSliderGrp -label "Color" -rgb 1 0 0;
```

Slider: Similar to a scrollbar, a slider is a tick bar that can be scrolled within a range of values. Sliders can represent floats, integers, and color. Slider groups are used to couple slider objects with text fields, buttons, and color swatches.

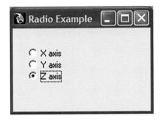

```
radioCollection;
radioButton -label "X axis"  -align "left";
```

Radio button: Users can choose only one radio button within a radio button collection. By choosing a button, any previously chosen button within the same collection will turn off. You can also create radio button groups that create one to four radio buttons in a single row, belonging to the same collection.

```
separator;
separator -style "none";
separator -style "single";
...
```

Separator: An aesthetic line that helps organize the interface. Styles of separators include the default, none, single, double, single dash, double dash, etched in, and etched out.

```
text -label "Simple Label";
```

Text: Creates a simple text label.

Expressions

Expressions are made from MEL commands and equations in order to drive animation or rig. The Expression Editor is accessed by choosing Window → Animation Editors → Expression Editor. This editor provides an artist-friendly interface to help build code that is constantly executed.

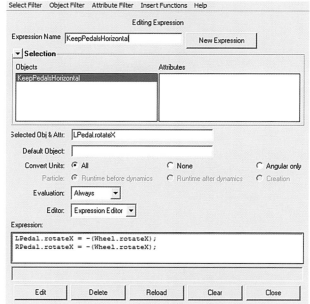

Particle expressions can be used to simulate changes to your particles over time. You can create complex changes in color, lifespan, and other particle attributes by using mathematical expressions and MEL.

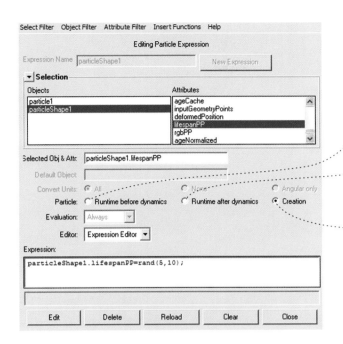

Expressions entered here will be evaluated before dynamics are applied to the particle.

Expressions entered here will be evaluated after dynamics are applied to the particle.

Expressions entered here will be evaluated just after the particle is created.

Procedures

Procedures allow you to encapsulate a series of MEL commands and to call them by a named function. Like MEL functions, procedures can take arguments and return values:

```
global proc MakeSpheres(int $num)
{
  while ($num > 0)
  {
    polySphere;
    move -r $num $num 0;
    $num-;
  }
};
```

To run a procedure, call its name and pass in parameters (if any):

```
MakeSpheres(5);
```

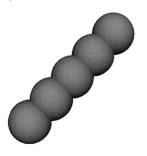

Creating Skeletons with Curves

A problem when building skeletons is that you cannot directly edit the position of joints without moving the children beneath them. This MEL script allows you to convert the CVs of a curve to joints in order to previsualize where a skeleton will be placed.

1 Open the Script Editor by choosing Window → General Editors → Script Editor.

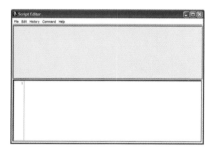

2 We'll begin by creating a global procedure so that we can execute the script by name.

```
global proc createSkeleton()
{
}
```

3 Because the script will need a selected curve, we can execute the List command with a selection flag, and assign the results to an array of strings.

```
global proc createSkeleton()
{
    // array of selected objects
    string $sel[] = `ls -sl`;
}
```

4 Now that we have an array of the user's selection, let's find the last object the user selected (for this example, we assume the user has selected a valid curve object). We can use the Size command to find the length of the selection array. Remember, array slots start at zero, so we need to subtract one from the size in order to get the index of the last element. Finally, we make a string variable, $curve, hold the name of the last user-selected object.

```
global proc createSkeleton()
{
    // array of selected objects
    string $sel[] = `ls -sl`;

    // name of the curve to convert
    int $lastSelect = size($sel) - 1;
    string $curve = $sel[$lastSelect];
}
```

5 Now that we have the curve, we need to find out how many CVs it has, because our goal is to create a joint on each one. The number of CVs in a curve equals the degree of the curve plus the number of spans. We can use the Get Attribute command to find these numbers and then assign their sum to a variable.

```
global proc createSkeleton()
{
  // array of selected objects
  string $sel[] = `ls -sl`;

  // name of the curve to convert
  int $lastSelect = size($sel) - 1;
  string $curve = $sel[$lastSelect];

  // find the number of CVs (Degree + Spans)
  int $numCVs = `eval("getAttr " + $curve + ".degree")` +
    `eval("getAttr " + $curve + ".spans")`;
}
```

6 Because we ultimately want to create a joint on each CV, we need to iterate through them all in order to extract their positional information. Create a standard for loop that iterates through the number of CVs.

```
global proc createSkeleton()
{
  // array of selected objects
  string $sel[] = `ls -sl`;

  // name of the curve to convert
  int $lastSelect = size($sel) - 1;
  string $curve = $sel[$lastSelect];

  // find the number of CVs (Degree + Spans)
  int $numCVs = `eval("getAttr " + $curve + ".degree")` +
    `eval("getAttr " + $curve + ".spans")`;

  // for each CV in the curve create a joint
  for ($i = 0; $i < $numCVs; $i++)
  {
  }
}
```

7 The first thing we need to do within the loop is figure out the coordinates of the current CV. The `pointPosition` command can do exactly that. We can build a string whose results, when evaluated, return a vector of three floats representing the X, Y, and Z coordinates of the current CV.

```
global proc createSkeleton()
{
  // array of selected objects
  string $sel[] = `ls -sl`;

  // name of the curve to convert
  int $lastSelect = size($sel) - 1;
  string $curve = $sel[$lastSelect];

  // find the number of CVs (Degree + Spans)
  int $numCVs = `eval("getAttr " + $curve + ".degree")` +
    `eval("getAttr " + $curve + ".spans")`;

  // for each CV in the curve create a joint
  for ($i = 0; $i < $numCVs; $i++)
  {
    // array to hold coordinates for each CV
    float $CVPosition[3];

    // find the current CV position
    $CVPosition = `eval("pointPosition " + $curve + ".cv[" + $i + "]")`;
  }
}
```

8 Now that we have captured the coordinates of the current CV, we can create a joint at the CV's position. We will name each joint by the curve's name plus the word *joint* plus the index number of the CV it relates to. In order for the `joint` command to work, we need to clear the selection. Do this just before the `for` loop.

```
global proc createSkeleton()
{
  // array of selected objects
  string $sel[] = `ls -sl`;

  // name of the curve to convert
  int $lastSelect = size($sel) - 1;
  string $curve = $sel[$lastSelect];
```

```
      // find the number of CVs (Degree + Spans)
      int $numCVs = `eval("getAttr " + $curve + ".degree")` +
        `eval("getAttr " + $curve + ".spans")`;

      // selection must be clear for joint command to work
      select -cl;

      // for each CV in the curve create a joint
      for ($i = 0; $i < $numCVs; $i++)
      {
        // array to hold coordinates for each CV
        float $CVPosition[3];

        // find the current CV position
        $CVPosition = `eval("pointPosition " + $curve + ".cv[" + $i + "]")`;

        joint -p $CVPosition[0] $CVPosition[1] $CVPosition[2]
            -n ($curve + "joint" + $i);
      }
    }
```

9 Although the numbering method in the previous step works, a more-appropriate naming convention calls its first joint in the chain Root and its last joint End. Create conditional if…else statements to figure out which CV we are evaluating, and then name it properly.

```
    global proc createSkeleton()
    {
      // array of selected objects
      string $sel[] = `ls -sl`;

      // name of the curve to convert
      int $lastSelect = size($sel) - 1;
      string $curve = $sel[$lastSelect];

      // find the number of CVs (Degree + Spans)
      int $numCVs = `eval("getAttr " + $curve + ".degree")` +
        `eval("getAttr " + $curve + ".spans")`;

      // selection must be clear for joint command to work
      select -cl;
```

```
         // for each CV in the curve create a joint
         for ($i = 0; $i < $numCVs; $i++)
         {
           // array to hold coordinates for each CV
           float $CVPosition[3];

           // find the current CV position
           $CVPosition = `eval("pointPosition " + $curve + ".cv[" + $i + "]")`;

           // if this is the first CV
           if ($i == 0)
           {
             joint -p $CVPosition[0] $CVPosition[1] $CVPosition[2]
                 -n ($curve + "jointRoot");
           }
           // if this is the last CV
           else if ($i == $numCVs - 1)
           {
             joint -p $CVPosition[0] $CVPosition[1] $CVPosition[2]
                 -n ($curve + "jointEnd");
           }
           // this CV is not beginning or end
           else
           {
             joint -p $CVPosition[0] $CVPosition[1] $CVPosition[2]
                 -n ($curve + "joint" + $i);
           }
         }
       }
```

10 When creating joints through MEL, they do not properly orient themselves to their parent joints. To reorient them, we will need to iterate through the joints. Create a for loop, but this time exclude the root and end joints by starting the loop at 1 and ending it at the number of CVs minus 1.

```
       global proc createSkeleton()
       {
         // array of selected objects
         string $sel[] = `ls -sl`;

         // name of the curve to convert
         int $lastSelect = size($sel) - 1;
         string $curve = $sel[$lastSelect];
```

```
// find the number of CVs (Degree + Spans)
int $numCVs = `eval("getAttr " + $curve + ".degree")` +
  `eval("getAttr " + $curve + ".spans")`;

// selection must be clear for joint command to work
select -cl;

// for each CV in the curve create a joint
for ($i = 0; $i < $numCVs; $i++)
{
  // array to hold coordinates for each CV
  float $CVPosition[3];

  // find the current CV position
  $CVPosition = `eval("pointPosition " + $curve + ".cv[" + $i + "]")`;

  // if this is the first CV
  if ($i == 0)
  {
    joint -p $CVPosition[0] $CVPosition[1] $CVPosition[2]
        -n ($curve + "jointRoot");
  }
  // if this is the last CV
  else if ($i == $numCVs - 1)
  {
    joint -p $CVPosition[0] $CVPosition[1] $CVPosition[2]
        -n ($curve + "jointEnd");
  }
  // this CV is not beginning or end
  else
  {
    joint -p $CVPosition[0] $CVPosition[1] $CVPosition[2]
        -n ($curve + "joint" + $i);
  }
}

// reorient joints
for ($i = 1; $i < ($numCVs - 1); $i++)
{
}

}
```

11 To edit the properties of an existing joint, we need to know it by name. Because we named them previously, we can easily figure out the name based on the current iteration of the for loop. After you have the name, select the current joint.

```
global proc createSkeleton()
{
  // array of selected objects
  string $sel[] = `ls -sl`;

  // name of the curve to convert
  int $lastSelect = size($sel) - 1;
  string $curve = $sel[$lastSelect];

  // find the number of CVs (Degree + Spans)
  int $numCVs = `eval("getAttr " + $curve + ".degree")` +
    `eval("getAttr " + $curve + ".spans")`;

  // selection must be clear for joint command to work
  select -cl;

  // for each CV in the curve create a joint
  for ($i = 0; $i < $numCVs; $i++)
  {
    // array to hold coordinates for each CV
    float $CVPosition[3];

    // find the current CV position
    $CVPosition = `eval("pointPosition " + $curve + ".cv[" + $i + "]")`;

    // if this is the first CV
    if ($i == 0)
    {
      joint -p $CVPosition[0] $CVPosition[1] $CVPosition[2]
          -n ($curve + "jointRoot");
    }
    // if this is the last CV
    else if ($i == $numCVs - 1)
    {
      joint -p $CVPosition[0] $CVPosition[1] $CVPosition[2]
          -n ($curve + "jointEnd");
    }
    // this CV is not beginning or end
    else
    {
      joint -p $CVPosition[0] $CVPosition[1] $CVPosition[2]
          -n ($curve + "joint" + $i);
    }
  }
```

```
// reorient joints
for ($i = 1; $i < ($numCVs - 1); $i++)
{
  // find the name of the current joint
  string $currentJoint = $curve + "joint" + $i;
  select $currentJoint;
}


}
```

12 To edit a joint's property, we can use the `joint` command with the edit flag. Then, set the flags to scale the orientation to 0 and orient the joint to xyz, which will orient it to its first child joint.

```
global proc createSkeleton()
{
  // array of selected objects
  string $sel[] = `ls -sl`;

  // name of the curve to convert
  int $lastSelect = size($sel) - 1;
  string $curve = $sel[$lastSelect];

  // find the number of CVs (Degree + Spans)
  int $numCVs = `eval("getAttr " + $curve + ".degree")` +
    `eval("getAttr " + $curve + ".spans")`;

  // selection must be clear for joint command to work
  select -cl;

  // for each CV in the curve create a joint
  for ($i = 0; $i < $numCVs; $i++)
  {
    // array to hold coordinates for each CV
    float $CVPosition[3];

    // find the current CV position
    $CVPosition = `eval("pointPosition " + $curve + ".cv[" + $i + "]")`;

    // if this is the first CV
    if ($i == 0)
    {
      joint -p $CVPosition[0] $CVPosition[1] $CVPosition[2]
          -n ($curve + "jointRoot");
    }
```

```
        // if this is the last CV
        else if ($i == $numCVs - 1)
        {
            joint -p $CVPosition[0] $CVPosition[1] $CVPosition[2]
                -n ($curve + "jointEnd");
        }
        // this CV is not beginning or end
        else
        {
            joint -p $CVPosition[0] $CVPosition[1] $CVPosition[2]
                -n ($curve + "joint" + $i);
        }
    }

    // reorient joints
    for ($i = 1; $i < ($numCVs - 1); $i++)
    {
        // find the name of the current joint
        string $currentJoint = $curve + "joint" + $i;
        select $currentJoint;

        // reorient the current joint
        joint -e -zeroScaleOrient -orientJoint xyz;
    }

}
```

13 Execute the script by typing Ctrl+Enter/⌘+Return, or by choosing Command → Execute. If there are any errors, be sure all of your syntax is correct. By executing this script, the command createSkeleton() is now available.

14 Create a curve and execute the createSkeleton() command to see the script in action.

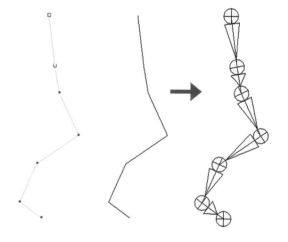

Index

Note to the Reader: Throughout this index boldfaced page numbers indicate primary discussions of a topic.

Wiley Publishing, Inc.
End-User License Agreement

READ THIS. You should carefully read these terms and conditions before opening the software packet(s) included with this book "Book". This is a license agreement "Agreement" between you and Wiley Publishing, Inc. "WPI". By opening the accompanying software packet(s), you acknowledge that you have read and accept the following terms and conditions. If you do not agree and do not want to be bound by such terms and conditions, promptly return the Book and the unopened software packet(s) to the place you obtained them for a full refund.

1. **License Grant.** WPI grants to you (either an individual or entity) a nonexclusive license to use one copy of the enclosed software program(s) (collectively, the "Software," solely for your own personal or business purposes on a single computer (whether a standard computer or a workstation component of a multi-user network). The Software is in use on a computer when it is loaded into temporary memory (RAM) or installed into permanent memory (hard disk, CD-ROM, or other storage device). WPI reserves all rights not expressly granted herein.

2. **Ownership.** WPI is the owner of all right, title, and interest, including copyright, in and to the compilation of the Software recorded on the physical packet included with this Book "Software Media". Copyright to the individual programs recorded on the Software Media is owned by the author or other authorized copyright owner of each program. Ownership of the Software and all proprietary rights relating thereto remain with WPI and its licensers.

3. **Restrictions On Use and Transfer.**

   (a) You may only (i) make one copy of the Software for backup or archival purposes, or (ii) transfer the Software to a single hard disk, provided that you keep the original for backup or archival purposes. You may not (i) rent or lease the Software, (ii) copy or reproduce the Software through a LAN or other network system or through any computer subscriber system or bulletin-board system, or (iii) modify, adapt, or create derivative works based on the Software.

   (b) You may not reverse engineer, decompile, or disassemble the Software. You may transfer the Software and user documentation on a permanent basis, provided that the transferee agrees to accept the terms and conditions of this Agreement and you retain no copies. If the Software is an update or has been updated, any transfer must include the most recent update and all prior versions.

4. **Restrictions on Use of Individual Programs.** You must follow the individual requirements and restrictions detailed for each individual program in the About the CD-ROM appendix of this Book or on the Software Media. These limitations are also contained in the individual license agreements recorded on the Software Media. These limitations may include a requirement that after using the program for a specified period of time, the user must pay a registration fee or discontinue use. By opening the Software packet(s), you will be agreeing to abide by the licenses and restrictions for these individual programs that are detailed in the About the CD-ROM appendix and/or on the Software Media. None of the material on this Software Media or listed in this Book may ever be redistributed, in original or modified form, for commercial purposes.

5. **Limited Warranty.**

   (a) WPI warrants that the Software and Software Media are free from defects in materials and workmanship under normal use for a period of sixty (60) days from the date of purchase of this Book. If WPI receives notification within the warranty period of defects in materials or workmanship, WPI will replace the defective Software Media.

   (b) WPI AND THE AUTHOR(S) OF THE BOOK DISCLAIM ALL OTHER WARRANTIES, EXPRESS OR IMPLIED, INCLUDING WITHOUT LIMITATION IMPLIED WARRANTIES OF MERCHANTABILITY AND FITNESS FOR A PARTICULAR PURPOSE, WITH RESPECT TO THE SOFTWARE, THE PROGRAMS, THE SOURCE CODE CONTAINED THEREIN, AND/OR THE TECHNIQUES DESCRIBED IN THIS BOOK. WPI DOES NOT WARRANT THAT THE FUNCTIONS CONTAINED IN THE SOFTWARE WILL MEET YOUR REQUIREMENTS OR THAT THE OPERATION OF THE SOFTWARE WILL BE ERROR FREE.

   (c) This limited warranty gives you specific legal rights, and you may have other rights that vary from jurisdiction to jurisdiction.

6. **Remedies.**

   (a) WPI's entire liability and your exclusive remedy for defects in materials and workmanship shall be limited to replacement of the Software Media, which may be returned to WPI with a copy of your receipt at the following address: Software Media Fulfillment Department, Attn.: *Maya 8 at a Glance*, Wiley Publishing, Inc., 10475 Crosspoint Blvd., Indianapolis, IN 46256, or call 1-800-762-2974. Please allow four to six weeks for delivery. This Limited Warranty is void if failure of the Software Media has resulted from accident, abuse, or misapplication. Any replacement Software Media will be warranted for the remainder of the original warranty period or thirty (30) days, whichever is longer.

   (b) In no event shall WPI or the author be liable for any damages whatsoever (including without limitation damages for loss of business profits, business interruption, loss of business information, or any other pecuniary loss) arising from the use of or inability to use the Book or the Software, even if WPI has been advised of the possibility of such damages.

   (c) Because some jurisdictions do not allow the exclusion or limitation of liability for consequential or incidental damages, the above limitation or exclusion may not apply to you.

7. **U.S. Government Restricted Rights.** Use, duplication, or disclosure of the Software for or on behalf of the United States of America, its agencies and/or instrumentalities "U.S. Government" is subject to restrictions as stated in paragraph (c)(1)(ii) of the Rights in Technical Data and Computer Software clause of DFARS 252.227-7013, or subparagraphs (c) (1) and (2) of the Commercial Computer Software - Restricted Rights clause at FAR 52.227-19, and in similar clauses in the NASA FAR supplement, as applicable.

8. **General.** This Agreement constitutes the entire understanding of the parties and revokes and supersedes all prior agreements, oral or written, between them and may not be modified or amended except in a writing signed by both parties hereto that specifically refers to this Agreement. This Agreement shall take precedence over any other documents that may be in conflict herewith. If any one or more provisions contained in this Agreement are held by any court or tribunal to be invalid, illegal, or otherwise unenforceable, each and every other provision shall remain in full force and effect.